Fire To Life: Africa's Biochar Potential Unleashed

How to Leverage African Biochar for Global Impact and Environmental Sustainability in One Year Without Struggling to Find Comprehensive Information.

Copyright Nawaz Khan © 2024

The right of Nawaz Khan to be identified as the author of this work has been asserted in accordance with the copyright designs and patent Act 1988

drjonathanfrost.com

ISBN: 9798323355488

Imprint: Independently published

All rights reserved. No part of this publication may be reproduced, stored in a retrieval system or transmitted in any form or by any means electronic, mechanical, photocopying, recording and/or otherwise without the prior written permission of the publishers. This book may not be lent, resold, hired out or otherwise disposed of by way of trading any form, binding or cover other than that in which it is published without the prior consent of the publishers.

Printed by Amazon

Table of Contents

Preface	1
Chapter 1: Unearthing the Power of Carbon Sequestration	6
Chapter 2: The Impact of Biochar on Soil Fertility	22
Chapter 3: Biochar and Soil Erosion Prevention	40
Chapter 4: Biochar's Contribution to Water Conservation	55
Chapter 5: Biochar for Sustainable Waste Management	70
Chapter 6: Biochar's Impact on Biodiversity	84
Chapter 7: Biochar Reduces Chemical Fertilizer Usage	95
Chapter 8: Biochar as a Renewable Energy Source	108
Chapter 9: Economic Opportunities from Biochar	124
Chapter 10: Biochar Mitigates Climate Change	145
Technical Notes	165
Successful Case Studies:	166

Acknowledgements

I appreciate discussions with Dr Jonathan Frost and Sue Cubberly.

I am happy and proud to acknowledge help and encouragement from Sean Vosler and the team at Movable Type.

Dedication

To All of You

Fire To Life

Preface

The best time to plant a tree was 20 years ago. The second best time is now. - African Proverb

This book is an invitation to join me on an extraordinary journey, one that holds the key to unlocking Africa's green potential. It is a guided tour through the transformative power of biochar and its role in environmental sustainability, promising to change the landscape of agriculture, climate change, and carbon sequestration. Fire To Life is your passport to understanding and leveraging the far-reaching impact of biochar, offering a comprehensive roadmap to a greener, more sustainable future for Africa and the world.

Imagine a world where carbon sequestration isn't just a lofty ambition, but a reality facilitated by natural, profitable, cost-effective solutions using current technology or much better technology made from locally available materials in third world countries. Picture a future where sustainable agriculture isn't a buzzword, but a thriving practice that nourishes the land and rural communities in equal measure whilst benefitting the world. This book is not merely an imagined utopia—it is a practical guide to making these visions a global reality based on experience and real life case studies.

As the Chief Operations Officer of Nature Based Solutions East Africa Ltd, I've witnessed countless individuals and organizations wrestling with the lack of accessible, comprehensive information on biochar. I've seen aspiring farmers and dedicated environmentalists in **Nairobi** and **Mombasa** struggle to find the guidance they need to leverage biochar effectively. I've talked to government officials in ministries and forestry departments, frustrated men and women with PhD's gathering dust. I've had to correct eminent Europeans on their lack of understanding on just how big a market this can be. Their frustration and determination to achieve results have become my driving force, compelling me to compile this definitive resource to bridge the practical knowledge gap and empower a wave of positive change.

I've had the privilege of working alongside passionate individuals with far greater knowledge than me, I cannot tell you how skilled the illiterate women and men we work with in making biochar are, they are literally modern-day alchemists, and can easily become committed to regenerating indigenous forests and grasslands, not just in Kenya, but across the African continent. Their unwavering dedication, coupled their manual labour, multiplied 10,000-fold with the potential for biochar to transform their efforts into a megaton-scale CO_2 removal mechanism, has ignited the fire within me to create this book. It's for the dreamers and the doers; those who yearn for a more sustainable future and are ready to roll up their sleeves and make it a reality. More importantly, for those in the EU, the USA, the UK, Japan and the Middle East who want to invest in something tangible that is a multiple-benefits incremental investment that is doable in one-tonne or 1,000 tonne lots, permanent for 1,000+ years.

The seeds of inspiration for this book were sown not only by my personal experiences but also by the collective wisdom and collaboration of experts, researchers, and community leaders who have tirelessly championed the cause of environmental sustainability. The illiterate peasant women who make charcoal deep in the forest, then walk three to four through the African bush carrying 35-40Kg sacks on their backs in the sweltering sun, their invaluable contributions and entrenched position in the value chain have fortified the foundation of this book, infusing it with the wealth of knowledge and practical expertise necessary to spark a revolution in biochar adoption and application on a Megatonne, even Gigatonne scale in the next few years.

To you, the reader, I extend my deepest gratitude. Your decision to invest your time in these pages is an affirmation of your commitment to positive change. I thank you for your trust and assure you that, within these chapters, you will find the answers, insights and indeed links you seek. Your journey through these words will equip you with the knowledge, strategies, and inspiration to not only understand biochar but to leverage its potential for monumental global impact and environmental sustainability.

Fire To Life

To the environmentally-conscious individuals, farmers, scientists, policymakers, and changemakers who seek a deeper understanding of biochar, this book is your guide. No prior expertise in biochar is required; all that's needed is an open mind and a readiness to embark on an enlightening and empowering journey. So, as you turn the page and journey through this book, know that you hold the key to unlocking Africa's green potential and making a lasting impact on the global stage.

Kenya is chosen as an example due to its geography entrepreneurial spirit and environmentally-aware leadership, what works in Kenya can be replicated all over Africa, at a much greater scale. Kenya produces between 2Mn to 4Mn tonnes of charcoal every year. If we bury it, it is biochar. For comparison, the European Biochar Consortium applauded itself for producing 50,000 tonnes biochar in 2022.

EU's GDP $17Trillion.

Kenya's GDP $113Bn.

The choice of candidate for any meaningful investments in Biochar is obvious.

Thank you for choosing this book. Now, let's venture forward and uncover the transformative power of biochar together.

Fire To Life

Each chapter has a preface – of what we want to see. This is not a dream – each story has been trialled on a small scale – successfully, now needs to be scaled up to Megatonne then Gigatonne level.

This is NOT a technical book, if you follow me on LinkedIn, you will find Dr Hamed Sanei and Hans Peter Schmidt, whose work is "down to atomic level if you want the theory behind biochar". Here is a paper that shows 76% of biochar is inertinite, 100million years+ stable in soil. I am happy just for 100 years down the road, enabling the next three generations some breathing space and figure out a new path for their descendants.

URL: sciencedirect.com/science/article/pii/S0166516223002276

Latest developments are noted on linkedin.com/in/nawazkhan66

Chapter 1: Unearthing the Power of Carbon Sequestration

Kamau stood amid the expanse of his Kenyan farm at the first light of dawn, his gaze drinking in the verdant sea of maize stretching to the horizon. The sun, a shy observer peeking over the distant Mau Hills, bathed his crops in warm hues of gold and amber. The earth beneath his feet, a canvas of the great Rift Valley, whispered tales of ancient, slumbering soil revitalized by a newfound ally—biochar.

As the chorus of the waking livestock punctuated the morning air, Kamau's mind wandered to the workshop he had attended mere weeks ago, where discussions of climate change, not as a distant threat but a past and ever-present adversary, had become the catalyst for change in his community. In that gathering of minds, biochar had been the recurring mantra—a beacon of hope in the discourse of carbon sequestration, a simple technology with mighty promises, one that could entwine the destinies of mankind with the land they so deeply cherished.

He mulled over how biochar, the darkest of soils yet bearer of life, could guard the carbon usually returned to the air and ensnare it within the earth's embrace for centuries. How the porous character of this charred organic remnant welcomed not only fungi but also microbes and nutrients into its microscopic nooks and crannies, transforming the tired ground into a bastion of fertility and microscopic life. His dreams swelled with the notion of Africa revising the narrative of climate change, wielding biochar as her pen to sketch a greener tomorrow.

Amidst Kamau's reverie, the murmur of voices drew near—his neighbours, eager to learn, see, touch, and eventually, to believe in this new technology. Witnessing their collective awakening to the significance of African biochar and its symphony with the environment was akin to watching the splendid marabou storks take flight—ungainly, uncoordinated and chaotic at first glance yet magnificent in unity when in flight, all flying off to distant destinations, arriving together for the feast. He remembered vividly the spark that had ignited within them as they connected the dots between local actions and global impacts, between their farms and the ever-growing role of carbon credits in the global economy.

And with that spark, the realization that carbon sequestration was not just another far-removed scientific term but a concrete step towards local wealth creation; not just an act of preservation but an active stride towards prosperity. They, the guardians of the Kenyan soil, could champion a movement grounded in ethics and practicality, where the earth's healing and their well-being sang the same tune.

But as the sun climbed higher and the day's labour beckoned, Kamau's optimism faced skirmishes with doubt. What if the grand potential of biochar did not unfurl as the scientists claimed? What if these efforts were insignificant ripples against the tide of global industrial emissions?

Yet, as the laughter and chatter of the community filled his senses, the worry ebbed. He knew the way forward was paved with such uncertainties, but it was the resolve to tread it that forged the path of champions. After all, revolutions and restorations began with the single act of one soul inspiring another, and charcoal making (now called pyrolysis) was something even his grandfather excelled at. How could he, who had been handling biochar since childhood, not succeed when challenged to mass-produce biochar?

In his heart, the rhythm of hope beat louder than the thrum of fear, and Kamau's spirit soared with resolve, as unstoppable as the sweeping winds over the savannahs.

Could this simple ubiquitous substance not only transform Kenyan soils but also the very fabric of our global ecosystem, rendering the battle against an ever-warming planet one that begins with a handful of charred earth?

Unearthing the Power of Carbon Sequestration

The true and deep understanding of biochar's potential to capture, store and lock away carbon in the soil creates a pivotal shift in climate change mitigation. This insight might seem counter-intuitive, but not only reveals the significance of biochar in combating global warming but also emphasizes the immense potential for African biochar to make a substantial impact on reducing carbon emissions. This chapter serves as a launching pad to explore the profound impact of biochar, particularly from Africa, in addressing one of the most pressing environmental challenges of our time: reducing CO_2 levels in our atmosphere by locking them underground as Carbon for 1,000+ years.

Amidst the urgency of climate change, the role of biochar in capturing and storing carbon in the soil is often overlooked yet holds incredible promise. By recognizing its true potential, we can pave the way for a sustainable and greener future. Biochar's capacity for long-term carbon sequestration offers a tangible solution to mitigate the hazardous effects of global warming, shifting us towards a more sustainable global ecosystem. This has been scientifically proved by Hans-Peter Schmidt and Hamed Sanei's work, and empirical evidence is provided by the Amazon's Terra Preta, at 2,000 years old.

In this chapter, we will delve into the significance of biochar in mitigating climate change through carbon sequestration. By understanding the mechanisms through which biochar captures and retains carbon in the soil, we can grasp its immense potential for combating global warming. Through exploration and introspection, we will uncover the intricate web of possibilities that biochar presents in the fight against climate change. It is indeed a complex solution to a complex problem, one that touches on many aspects of human life.

Furthermore, we will shine a light on how African biochar contributes to reducing carbon emissions and combating global warming, especially by preventing natural generation of methane, a gas said to be 30X (UNEP says 80X) more deadly than CO_2 for global warming. The discussion will illuminate the unique advantages that African biochar brings to the forefront and how it can play a pivotal role in addressing global environmental challenges.

This crucial chapter sets the stage for the transformative journey ahead, opening our eyes to the untapped potential of biochar in Africa.

Africa is uniquely placed in the potential for gigatonne-scale removal of CO_2. Europe has billions of trees, each and every one has a purpose waiting – paper or furniture, there is no spare biomass, nor spare land. North America has billions of tonnes to spare, but labour costs are very high and they have no spare land in as much as it takes a decade to approve large scale land-use projects, due to lawsuits by interested parties. Africa is unique in that is has billions of tonnes of waste biomass, low labour costs, lots of water resources and spare land available, a unique coincidence of what-we-want, what-we-need, that gives it an unbeatable competitive advantage.

Fire To Life

Within Africa, Kenya's leadership makes it a vanguard in this charge to reduce CO_2 in the atmosphere.

By harnessing the power of carbon sequestration, the Biochar Revolution in Africa stands poised to make a lasting impact on the global economy, create local wealth, and significantly contribute to environmental sustainability. Our exploration of biochar will unlock the doors to a world of possibilities, empowering us to leverage African biochar for global change. Through this, we will grasp the incredible potential that biochar possesses to pave the way for a more sustainable future for humankind.

Join me on this journey as we unlock the potential of carbon sequestration and explore the myriad possibilities that African biochar holds for global impact and environmental sustainability. Together, we will unfold the transformative power of biochar and pave the way for a greener, more sustainable future for us all.

Understanding the role of biochar in capturing and storing carbon in the soil is crucial to comprehending its potential for combating climate change. Biochar, is essentially defined as a type of high temperature charcoal produced from organic materials that will be buried. It has the unique ability to lock carbon in the soil for millennia. This process, known as carbon sequestration, is a powerful tool in the fight against global warming. By keeping carbon out of the atmosphere, biochar not only helps mitigate climate change but also enhances soil fertility and agricultural productivity.

The significance of biochar as a permanent carbon sequestration solution cannot be overstated. The soil's capacity to store carbon is immense, and biochar plays a pivotal role in enhancing this capability. When biochar is incorporated into the soil, it creates a stable environment for carbon storage, reducing the amount of greenhouse gases in the atmosphere by locking carbon underground and not releasing it back again. This has far-reaching environmental benefits, including mitigating climate change, improving soil health, and bolstering agricultural resilience.

This is very different to trees and old-growth forests, whose leaf fall is all eaten and digested by insects and fungi, metabolized then turned back into methane and CO_2 in a matter of years.

Think of old growth forests as steady-state "historical carbon vaults", and biochar as new deposits into the vault.

In the context of African biochar, the potential to contribute significantly to reducing carbon emissions is considerable. The rich agricultural landscapes of Kenya, for example, present an opportunity for widespread biochar implementation, further amplifying the impact of carbon sequestration. Imagine the vast expanses of soils in the villages and towns surrounding Nairobi, Mombasa, or Kisumu working as long-term carbon sinks, transforming the fight against climate change within local communities and beyond. The reason we say "villages and farms surrounding" is that we need to consider the carbon footprint for market farming – they need to be reasonably close to the cities – for reasons of freshness and logistics. Also in case of "verification of biochar concentration levels" the lands surrounding major cities are more accessible to any future auditors. The ability to prove at random unannounced dates by independent auditors (and satellites 24-7 if needs be) is the cornerstone of Carbon Credits and their most important characteristic if they are to be valuable and marketable – Trust. With auditors and satellites – this element of trust is reinforced and verified.

The power of biochar's carbon sequestration capabilities underscores its potential as a driver of change on a global scale. Carbon credits have become a valuable commodity in the global economy, and the role of biochar in generating these credits cannot be overlooked. As more emphasis is placed on sustainable practices and environmental responsibility, the ethical and practical aspects of local wealth creation come to the forefront. The wealth of a nation begins with the health of its soil, and biochar offers a sustainable means to enrich both the environment and local economies. The simple fact is, Direct air capture (DAC) and such technologies are energy consuming. Making biochar is an exothermic exercise, the kilns are energy producing.

I have to point out early in this book, most studies on biochar quote 1-2 tonnes per acre/hectare, whereas trials of vegetable grown in 100% biochar are showing good results. The Swedes quoted in chapter 2 used 2,800Kg per hectare to show remarkable results in productivity. Amazonian Terra Preta shows 9% biochar content, so common sense (to be tested in real world trials) suggests 1,300 tonnes per acre dug into the soil to a depth of 1 metre is not unreasonable.

Read on, to explore how African biochar contributes to reducing carbon emissions and combating global warming.

The significance of biochar in mitigating climate change through carbon sequestration cannot be overstated. As we journey towards understanding the potentially profound impact of biochar, it is essential to recognize its pivotal role in capturing and storing carbon in the soil. On this path of discovery, we unearth the power of biochar to combat global warming by keeping carbon and methane out of the atmosphere.

Biochar mixed and buried into the top layer of landfills will host methane metabolizing bacteria which will reduce CH_4 leakages into the atmosphere. Biochar mixed in with cattle feed also, in tests, has reduced the amount of methane cows emit. This insight not only promises to address one of the key environmental challenges of our time but also offers a beacon of hope for a sustainable future.

Globally, the importance of carbon sequestration through biochar is becoming increasingly apparent. As the global economy places greater value on carbon credits, the role of biochar in capturing and storing carbon underground becomes more prominent. This shift opens up opportunities for local wealth creation and community empowerment. Through embracing the ethical and practical aspects of biochar production, African communities can find sustainable solutions to environmental challenges while also contributing to the global effort to combat climate change.

The sustainable production of biochar has the potential to transform rural communities, especially in Kenya, by creating opportunities for local wealth creation and economic growth. As the world increasingly recognizes the value of carbon credits, the demand for biochar as a means of carbon sequestration grows. African communities can capitalize on this demand by modernising and leveraging their centuries' old biochar production methods to positively impact the environment and generate local wealth. A simple modern kiln, locally produced by basically skilled artisans will improve the biochar output by 200% to 350% when compared to traditional methods of making biochar.

For the purposes of this book we will not discuss torrefaction, or any high-tech production method that requires anything more than a $10 hand-held thermometer and cannot be repaired in the bush using hammers, nails, screws and pop-rivets.

Furthermore, the significance of biochar in mitigating climate change goes beyond its role in capturing and storing carbon. Its impact extends to enhancing soil fertility, promoting sustainable agriculture, and fostering environmental sustainability and food security in African communities. By integrating biochar into agricultural practices, communities can enhance soil health, increase crop yields, and reduce the need for chemical fertilizers. This not only benefits local farmers but also has a positive impact on the environment by minimizing the use of environmentally harmful chemicals. It might seem paradoxical to most, but Africa's established agricultural zones have very badly eroded, nutrient-depleted soils, having been farmed for 50+ years using chemical fertilizers and pesticides, some are proven carcinogenic in the USA.

As we delve deeper into the significance of biochar, it becomes clear that its potential to mitigate climate change is intertwined with its ability to uplift communities and enhance ecosystems. The impact of biochar transcends environmental benefits, offering a pathway for communities to thrive while contributing to a global effort to combat climate change. The significance of biochar in mitigating climate change is not merely theoretical; it is a practical, actionable solution that offers hope for a sustainable future for African communities and the world at large. Since excess CO_2 is a 'common bad', what benefits Africa, benefits the world.

Fire To Life

The contribution of African biochar to reducing carbon emissions and combating global warming cannot be overlooked. In the villages surrounding Kenyan cities, the potential for biochar to make a significant impact on climate change is becoming increasingly evident. Harnessing the power of biochar in carbon sequestration presents an opportunity not only for environmental sustainability but also for economic empowerment within local communities. The significant role of Africa, particularly Kenya, in the global economy through the production of biochar and the trading of carbon credits is a trend that cannot be ignored.

The creation of carbon credits through biochar production presents a practical and ethical approach to local wealth creation. By incentivizing and monetizing sustainable practices, such as biochar production, through the trading of carbon credits, communities in Kenyan villages and agricultural towns can foster economic growth while contributing to the global effort to combat climate change. This creates a positive ripple effect, where local wealth creation aligns with global environmental sustainability efforts.

As the world grapples with the challenges posed by climate change, the role of biochar in capturing and storing carbon is gaining recognition. African biochar, with its unique properties and potential for large-scale production, can play a pivotal role in global carbon sequestration efforts. By highlighting the importance of African biochar, particularly from Kenyan communities and villages where biomass is abundant in reducing carbon emissions, we can inspire a renewed focus on leveraging this valuable human and biological resource for the benefit of both local communities and the planet.

The ethical implications of integrating biochar production into sustainable agriculture and land management practices cannot be overstated. By adopting biochar in Kenyan villages, rural communities, ranches and beyond, we can mitigate the adverse effects of climate change and restore soil health while empowering local farmers. This presents an opportunity to strengthen the resilience of communities against the impacts of a changing climate, while also contributing to global efforts to reduce carbon emissions and combat global warming.

The growing role of carbon credits in the global economy further underscores the significance of African biochar in reducing carbon emissions. By participating in carbon credit trading, Kenyan communities can position themselves as key players in the global effort to address climate change. The ethical and practical implications of this approach cannot be underestimated, as it presents a pathway to sustainable economic development at grassroots level while simultaneously contributing to environmental preservation on a global scale.

Empowering local communities in Kenyan villages and towns to engage in biochar production not only fosters environmental sustainability but also promotes economic self-reliance. There are many impoverished parts of Kenya where this economic activity will create employment and bring about stability as poor armed folk turn their energy to working for money rather than cattle raiding as a rational economic activity. By investing in biochar production and prompting its integration into agricultural practices, the potential to drive positive change in both local economies and the global climate at scale becomes palpable. It's imperative to recognize the interconnectedness of these efforts and their potential to create a sustainable future for generations to come, through the simple practical act of burying biochar in Africa, the Taj Mahal in India and the Black Forest in Germany suffer less damage from acid rain.

The power of African biochar in reducing carbon emissions and combating global warming lies not only in its environmental impact but also in its capacity to elevate poor rural African communities. By harnessing the potential of biochar in Kenyan communities, villages and beyond, we can pave the way for a more sustainable and prosperous future. This is a pivotal moment to seize the opportunity presented by biochar and its role in mitigating climate change, local wealth creation, and global environmental sustainability.

The journey we've embarked upon in this chapter illustrates the transformative power of **carbon sequestration** through biochar. The potential impact of this age-old technique on combatting climate change and promoting environmental sustainability cannot be overstated. With every passing year, as the urgency of reducing carbon emissions grows more acute, the significance of biochar in capturing and storing carbon in soil permanently becomes increasingly pronounced. As we move forward in this book, the potential harvest of knowledge and action awaits us, one rich with the fruit of African biochar and its pivotal role in the fight against climate change.

The future promises to be a tapestry of accomplishments woven from the threads of sustainable practices, robust ecosystems, and empowered communities. In our quest to understand the extraordinary power of biochar, we have uncovered a pathway that leads to not only reduced carbon emissions but also to the prosperous enrichment of local communities. The vision of leveraging African biochar for global impact is not a distant dream; it's an achievable reality that is rooted in the very soil we tread upon, since we Africans have been making biochar for 1,000+ years and Kenya already produces two million tonnes. By unlocking the full potential of biochar to reduce atmospheric CO_2 through the financial markets, we ensure a future where a healthier planet coexists harmoniously with thriving communities, and where sustainable practices converge with economic empowerment.

As we delve into the wealth of knowledge and strategies to **leverage African biochar** for global impact, we are poised to witness the convergence of environmentalism and economic prosperity. The emergence of carbon credits in the global economy presents an opportunity for African nations, like Kenya, to not only actively participate but also lead in the global effort to combat climate change. The ethical imperative of local wealth creation is reinforced by the practical benefits of sustainable practices. At the heart of our exploration is the preservation of our planet and the uplifting of communities, where each individual becomes a custodian of a greener, more prosperous world.

As we stand on the threshold of this remarkable journey (back to safety), let us approach it with open minds and responsive hearts. The potential for change is not a distant mirage but a tangible reality waiting to be embraced and nurtured. In the chapters that lay ahead, we will learn how to harness the power of biochar to effect positive change, not only in our immediate surroundings but also on a global scale. The transformative potential of biochar is ours to unlock, and the bountiful harvest of knowledge and action awaits us. The time when a family in Luxembourg or Los Angeles pays a family in Africa to lock away 100 tonnes of CO_2 as biochar for their annual reduction should not be too far away.

Chapter 2: The Impact of Biochar on Soil Fertility

The sun cast long shadows across the Kenyan plains as it began to dip closer to the horizon, and there, in the outskirts of Nairobi a bustling modern city surrounded by the echoes of wildlife and whispering savannah grasses, was Mukora. Most nights he can see the lights of the capital reflecting off the night sky. Today he walked with a sense of purpose, his eyes reflecting the determined spirit of his people—a people constantly innovating to conquer the hunger that often gnawed at the edges of their lives, repeated failed harvests compounding his familial and communal poverty. The weight of food insecurity was a persistent thread woven into the fabric of his community since the 1970's, and today, it pulled tighter than ever. Food poverty is reality for many Kenyan farmers, few have any surplus goats or cows to sell, three years of drought (2020 to 2023) has seen to that, the bank savings account that was the herd of cows or goats was sold off to pay for school fees, uniforms, and medical bills from some aged relative's stay in hospital and subsequent funeral.

Mukora had recently learned of a material called biochar, a charcoal-like substance that some hailed as a miracle for revitalized soils. He understood that if the fertility of African soil could be enhanced, it could propel his agrarian society into a new era of food sustainability. As he navigated the crowded streets of this satellite town, heavy with the scent of roasting maize and exhaust from badly tuned vehicles, he contemplated the potential of this ancient yet largely untapped technology. In his mind's eye, he saw fields of maize reaching up towards the sun, robust and green, where once there had only been stunted, brittle yellow stalks.

He paused by a small market, the colours of fresh vegetable produce a stark contrast to the red dust that seemed permanently etched into the landscape of Machakos town. A conversation with a local farmer had ignited a quiet ember within him. The vision of biochar-enriched soils yielding more harvests each year could reshape their future, could challenge the persistent spectre of hunger that loomed over their children. It wasn't just about growing food; it was about restoring dignity and creating local wealth amidst the global economy's shifting stance on carbon credits, an opportunity to be prioritized and seized fervently. Many of his tribesmen had to work in the big cities doing menial jobs as askaris (security guards) and tyre-puncture repair men to make ends meet and send back a portion of their salaries to the wives and children in the village so they could eat.

Inside a tiny café, Mukora shared his thoughts with a group of young innovators, his words punctuated by the clatter of dishes and the hum of hopeful conversations. He spoke of the ethical implications, the capacity to create wealth not just for a few, but for an entire community, and then the entire nation. He described the practicality of biochar, how it required minimal technology, how their grandfather and fathers knew how to make it, and could be easily integrated into local agricultural practices. They listened, their expressions a shifting tapestry of curiosity, incredulousness and yet, he could see some resolve.

The discussion soon turned to the greater implications of their actions—how their toil could diminish the carbon footprint of their agriculture and attract international investors directly interested in ethical initiatives that combat climate change at grass-roots level. The possibility of harnessing carbon credits as a financial incentive energized the room. They envisioned a scenario where restoring their lands could simultaneously draw wealth and investment into their communities.

As the evening drew closer to night, and the air cooled to embrace the African darkness, Mukora walked home, the soil under his shoes somehow feeling more significant, more alive with potential. A cat darted across the path carrying a squirrel in its mouth, its sleek movement home a reminder of the adaptability of nature, and he couldn't help but smile at the thought of his people, as resilient as the land they cultivated, moving toward a future where hunger was a memory and prosperity a reality.

He lay in bed that night, the distant lights and sounds of Nairobi an ever-present siren song lullaby, pondering the days and decisions that lay ahead. How would the introduction of biochar shift the delicate balance of his society? What new dreams could take root in soil made fertile not just with nutrients, but with innovation and hope? Could the whispers of the past provide the answers they so desperately sought? And would the earth, which had borne witness to so many cycles of poor growth, defeat and decay, now become their steadfast partner in carving out a future that was truly their own?

Unleashing African Biochar: A Sustainable Solution for Soil Fertility

In a continent where agricultural productivity and food security is closely tied to the health of the soil, the potential of African biochar to enhance soil fertility stands as a beacon of hope. Chapter 2 of "Fire To Life: Africa's Biochar Potential Unleashed " delves deep into the impact of African biochar on soil fertility, shedding light on its transformative role in revitalizing depleted soils and promoting sustainable agricultural practices.

African Biochar's Capability: The capability of African biochar to enhance soil fertility and improve agricultural productivity is nothing short of revolutionary. Through its ability to sequester carbon and enrich the soil with vital nutrients, biochar presents a sustainable and cost-effective solution to combat soil degradation. By unlocking the potential of biochar, farming communities across Kenya, from Kisumu to Mombasa, have the opportunity to transform their agricultural landscapes and secure food sources for generations to come.

Revitalizing Depleted Soils: The chapter intricately examines how biochar breathes new life into depleted soils, creating a fertile environment for crops to thrive. By effectively retaining water and essential nutrients, biochar mitigates the impact of droughts and enhances the overall resilience of agricultural ecosystems. This revival of the soil not only fosters sustainable agricultural practices but also empowers farming communities to break free from the shackles of dwindling productivity, ushering in an era of prosperity and abundance. There is evidence that biochar-inoculated soil makes its own fertilizer, but we have discounted this for all practical farming purposes.

Promoting Sustainable Food Production: Perhaps most crucially, the chapter underscores the pivotal role of biochar in promoting sustainable food production and addressing food insecurity. With a rapidly growing population and the looming spectre of climate change, the need for sustainable and resilient agricultural practices has never been more pressing. African biochar emerges as a beacon of hope, offering a pathway to not just sustain but thrive in the face of environmental challenges.

This chapter in "Fire To Life" is a testament to the transformative potential of African biochar. It serves as a clarion call for communities across Kenya and beyond to embrace this sustainable solution, uplifting ecosystems and fostering prosperity. As we leverage the power of biochar, we not only nurture the soil but also cultivate a future where abundance and sustainability go hand in hand.

The capability of African biochar to enhance soil fertility is a game-changer for struggling agricultural communities. Biochar is initially charged then dug in, essentially injecting fertility directly, and releasing nutrients when needed, better water retention, and indeed – better adsorption of chemical fertilizers, less runoff and wastage. By understanding the impact of biochar on soil fertility, we can revitalize depleted soils using both organic manure and chemical fertilizers (Urea CAN NPK et. al.) and unlock the potential for sustainable agricultural practices. This insight is significant, not only for improving crop yields but also for addressing food insecurity and promoting environmental sustainability, since there is less fertilizer runoff in soils inoculated with biochar with biochar. Picture this: outside cities like Nairobi, Mombasa, and Kisumu, the impact of biochar on soil fertility in the farming communities surrounding the cities is transforming the way communities approach agriculture, cultivating fertile ground for a brighter, more sustainable future as crop harvests increase and crop quality increases.

Fire To Life

African biochar has the remarkable ability to improve the fertility of degraded soils, offering a sustainable solution to enhance agricultural productivity. With agricultural communities facing the challenge of depleted soils, the role of biochar cannot be overstated. In Kenyan villages, rural communities are witnessing first-hand the revitalization of barren lands as biochar breathes new life into the earth. The impact is tangible: increased crop yields, improved soil structure, and the mitigation of greenhouse gas emissions. The evidence is clear: African biochar is not just a remedy for degraded soils; it is a catalyst for agricultural productivity and environmental resilience.

Sweden's Lund University in 2019, applied from 1,000Kg to 10,000Kg per hectare at several locations in Kenya, here are the findings.

Kwale: Maize yields increased from 900Kg per hectare to 4,410Kg per hectare over several seasons.

Siaya: Maize yields increased from 2,900Kg per hectare to 3,900Kg per hectare over several seasons.

The researchers found that the biochar-charged soil had fewer deleterious fungi and more beneficial microbes, and more single-celled organisms called protists that enhance plant growth and improve plant health. There is no mention of "negative correlation between biochar dosing rates and crop yield", up to 10 tonnes per hectare.

Examining how biochar revitalizes depleted soils unveils a narrative of hope and progress. Communities in Kenya are embracing sustainable agricultural practices, thanks to the transformational power of biochar. The story of how biochar is nurturing once-barren lands and turning them into fertile havens is as inspirational as it is urgent. We cannot afford to overlook the role of biochar in creating sustainable food production systems to address the challenges of food insecurity and environmental degradation.

Understanding the role of biochar in promoting sustainable food production underscores its impact on global agriculture and ecosystems. From Nairobi to Mombasa, the demand for sustainable agriculture practices is gaining momentum, as is the need for fertile soils. Imported fertilizer is becoming increasingly expensive, and so manure is gaining importance, as well as reduced wastage from chemical fertilizers. African biochar stands at the intersection of these burgeoning needs, offering not just a solution to soil fertility challenges, but also a pathway to sustainable food production. The potential for biochar to create a positive impact on the environment and agricultural communities cannot be overstated, and its role in addressing global food insecurity is becoming increasingly vital.

Join us as we delve deeper into the transformative impact of African biochar on soil fertility and agricultural productivity in Kenyan villages. Let's explore the practical applications of biochar and how it is nurturing sustainable food production systems, one fertile soil system at a time.

Biochar is a powerful tool in revitalizing depleted soils and supporting sustainable agricultural practices, especially in Kenya. In regions where soils have been exhausted by years of intensive farming, the application of charged (see technical note1 at the end of the book) African biochar can restore fertility and productivity. This sustainable solution not only benefits local farmers but also enhances ecosystems and contributes to the global effort to combat climate change. The impact of biochar on agriculture has been well-documented, with studies showing significant improvements in soil structure, nutrient retention, and crop yields. By understanding how biochar revitalizes depleted soils and supports sustainable agricultural practices, we can unlock its full potential and bring about positive change in communities across Kenya.

The use of biochar has shown remarkable results in increasing soil fertility and agricultural productivity in various regions of Kenya. By incorporating biochar into the soil, farmers can improve water retention, reduce nutrient leaching, improve fertilizer utilization rates (less runoff) and enhance the availability of essential nutrients for plant growth. There is evidence that 'well-matured well-formulated' biochar in the soil actively generates soil nutrients, and it has been reported in the amazon, Terra Preta once sold off, regenerates in 20 years or so as fertile soil. This is apparently due to the fungi, microbes and microscopic insects that make the hollow biochar cells their home. This translates to healthier, more resilient crops and sustainable agricultural practices. With the increasing pressure on agricultural resources and the need for sustainable farming methods, biochar offers a viable solution to address these challenges while promoting eco-friendly practices.

Moreover, the holistic impact of biochar extends beyond soil fertility and agriculture. By supporting the adoption of biochar in agricultural practices, we can also promote environmental sustainability and combat climate change. The permanent (1,000+ years) sequestration of carbon in the soil through biochar application plays a crucial role in mitigating greenhouse gas emissions, contributing to the global effort to combat climate change. As the world embraces carbon credits and environmental accountability, the implementation of biochar in Kenyan agriculture can open up opportunities for local wealth creation through the sale of carbon credits while simultaneously benefitting the environment.

This sustainable solution not only addresses the immediate challenges of soil degradation, agricultural productivity and increased food security, but also aligns with the global movement towards environmentally conscious practices. By integrating biochar into agricultural systems, we can foster a more ethical, practical, and sustainable approach to local wealth creation. This not only empowers local farmers to improve their livelihoods but also contributes to the broader goal of building resilient and sustainable agricultural ecosystems in Kenya, since their soil's ability to bury carbon adds value to the soil.

As we delve deeper into the role of biochar in revitalizing depleted soils and supporting sustainable agricultural practices, it becomes evident that this eco-friendly approach offers a myriad of benefits. By harnessing the potential of biochar, we can address the pressing issue of soil degradation, enhance agricultural productivity, and contribute to the larger global effort to combat climate change. The impact of biochar is not limited to the farms and fields of Kenya; it has the potential to resonate on a global scale, shaping the future of sustainable agriculture and environmental stewardship. Let us continue to explore the transformative power of biochar and the opportunities it presents for creating a more sustainable and prosperous future for communities across Kenya and beyond.

African Biochar and Sustainable Food Production

African biochar plays a pivotal role in promoting sustainable food production and addressing food insecurity. By unlocking the potential of biochar to revitalize degraded soils, communities across Kenya are witnessing a renaissance in agricultural productivity.

Sustainable food production is not just a theoretical concept; it directly impacts the livelihoods of countless individuals, fostering a brighter future for farmers and communities.

Understanding the Framework

The framework for biochar production methods is crucial in understanding the diverse techniques used to create biochar. The step-by-step process for each method, including pyrolysis and gasification, (for the purpose of this book we exclude torrefaction and hydrothermal carbonization or anything that requires computers and electronics to work), provides valuable insights into the intricacies involved. By highlighting the advantages and disadvantages of each production method in a Kenyan/African context, the framework empowers readers to make informed decisions based on their specific needs and resources and geography. In the EU and Scandinavia, a much more complex and sophisticated method of production may well prove to be more efficient. We are only considering "third world, specifically Kenya".

Role of Each Component

Each component of the biochar production framework serves a critical role in the overall process. Pyrolysis, using the traditional method, involves heating biomass in the partial absence of oxygen, resulting in biochar and syngas. This is done using a TEK –

traditional earth kiln: build a mound of dry wood, cover it with leaves, then soil, and set fire using controlled air flow. Gasification involves partial combustion of biomass to produce a hydrogen-rich gas, which can be used as a fuel, as seen in retort kilns Sophisticated production methods such as Torrefaction and Hydrothermal Carbonization, on the other hand, employ heat and pressure to convert biomass into biochar under specific conditions. Each method contributes to the creation of biochar and offers distinct benefits to the production process, especially increased yield, far in excess of third world methods.

Dynamics and Practical Implications

Understanding the dynamics of each biochar production method is essential for optimizing its application in sustainable food production in any particular country. By recognizing how these methods behave under different geographical conditions, farmers and stakeholders can leverage biochar to enhance soil fertility and promote crop yield. The practical implications are far-reaching, as the utilization of biochar directly influences the long-term sustainability of local agriculture and supports communities in advancing their food security objectives.

Enhancing Local Wealth Creation

The production and application of biochar not only support sustainable food production but also have a profound impact on local wealth creation. There is a double-economic benefit. The biochar producers find gainful employment, and burying biochar enables farmers to improve their crop yield and soil fertility, thus biochar becomes a catalyst for economic empowerment at the grassroots level both for the producer community and the end-user farmers. The ripple effect extends to the entire community, fostering economic resilience and securing livelihoods at both ends of the value chain, from producer to end-user. As the demand for biochar continues to rise, the economic value it generates contributes to a sustainable and prosperous future for multiple communities and players along the value chain, all the way up to global communities trying to reduce CO_2 in the atmosphere.

Ethical Considerations and Contribution to Ecosystems

The ethical dimension of cultivating biomass for biochar as a resource cannot be overlooked. It represents a holistic approach to agricultural practices, aiming to benefit both the environment and local communities, rebuilding degraded soils, wastelands and overall improved food security through income generation and side crops on the now improved lands. Through the utilization of biomass for biochar, farmers and stakeholders exhibit a deep commitment to enhancing ecosystems and uplifting themselves and their communities. This ethical foundation underlines the profound impact that biochar has in shaping a more sustainable agricultural landscape in Kenya.

Opportunities for Future Development and Application

As we delve into the framework and dynamics of biochar production, delivery and utilization methods, it's essential to recognize the vast opportunities for future development and application, not just in the growing, but in a new zero-carbon system of e-logistics, from harvesting, to final transport to end-user for burial. The advancements in biochar technology pave the way for innovative solutions that can further amplify its impact on sustainable food production and logistics. By examining the various components of the model, we can identify extra areas for improvement and innovation, creating a roadmap for continued progress in harnessing the potential of biochar for sustainable agriculture, as well as providing the impetus required to start a new line of e-equipment, e-bikes, e-tuktuks, and the ancillary support and generation equipment required.

In summary, the framework for biochar production methods illuminates the path towards sustainable food production and the alleviation of food insecurity, either through providing employment, or by providing better crop yields, ceteris paribus. By delving into the intricacies of each method and understanding their role, dynamics, and practical implications, we can harness the power of biochar to propel local wealth creation, enhance ecosystems, improve e-logistics and foster a sustainable agricultural landscape. This framework not only informs but also inspires the pursuit of innovative solutions that will lay the foundation for a thriving innovative agricultural sector in Kenya and beyond. The skills, techniques, failures, successes and lessons learned in this field will carry over into mainstream agriculture and transport logistics.

In understanding the transformative power of African biochar, it becomes abundantly clear that **soil fertility improvement** is not just a concept, but a tangible reality with far-reaching implications, "it punches above its weight". The capacity of biochar to enhance soil fertility and bolster agricultural productivity presents an unparalleled opportunity to create sustainable change, particularly in the context of addressing food insecurity. By revitalizing depleted soils and promoting sustainable practices, biochar emerges as a beacon of hope for communities grappling with environmental degradation and agricultural challenges, as well as ushering in a new generation of clean technology.

It is imperative to recognize that the impact of biochar extends far beyond merely improving soil quality. This unassuming substance has the potential to ignite a revolution in agricultural practices, leading to a self-sustaining cycle of prosperity. By promoting the integration of biochar into farming techniques, we are not only enhancing ecosystems but also bolstering local economies. The uptake of biochar as a means to improve soil fertility ushers in a new era of local wealth creation, overseas investment empowering communities to take control of their agricultural destinies.

Furthermore, as we navigate the landscape of global environmental initiatives, it is vital to acknowledge the growing role of **carbon credits** in the global economy and their capacity to transform the flow of funding and financing for effective CO_2 removal. The adoption of biochar in agricultural practices presents a compelling case for the generation of carbon credits, serving as a testament to the ethical and practical aspects of leveraging local resources for positive global impact. In doing so, we have the chance to weave a tapestry of sustainability, built upon the pillars of environmental stewardship and economic empowerment.

Through regenerating once fertile ground with African biochar, we stand on the threshold of a new era, one where sustainable food production and enhanced soil fertility converge to create flourishing landscapes. This journey carries with it the promise of transformative systemic change, from tractors to lorries to solar charging stations, biomass burial sites, biochar is poised to uplift communities and ecosystems alike. As we continue to explore the possibilities of biochar, let us remain steadfast in our commitment to fostering a greener, more prosperous future for all, ushering in new technologies. It makes no sense to be sequestering carbon permanently as buried biochar, and using fossil-fuelled equipment and machinery to do it in the long term. We must also seek to decarbonize the process, and logistics. Though outside the scope of this book – it is a necessary investment, which in itself will be a viable business line in future.

Chapter 3: Biochar and Soil Erosion Prevention

Korie Maru brushed the red soil off her knees, standing tall against the backdrop of endless farmland that stretched to meet the sky at the horizon. It was mid-afternoon, and the cicadas mounted their daily symphony, high-pitched and persistent, taking over where the crickets had mounted their discordant cacophony at night, the sun was a relentless watcher in the vast, blue expanse. Her mind was a patchwork of concern and determination; the land beneath her boots, once teeming with life, now cracked and thirsty, yearning for redemption.

In the folds of her memory, Korie Maru recalled the stories her grandmother told of how the earth used to cling to the roots like a mother to her child, firm yet nurturing. African grandmothers did most of the farming back then, from the heavy labour of digging to weeding to the back breaking weeding and harvesting. Erosion had been a stranger in those tales. But today, each heavy rain was a thief, stealing the soil from her ancestral lands, the winds abetting in the crime. The land's cries had become a silent din in Maru's ears, playing over and over, a lament that begged for action.

She remembered the conference she attended in Nairobi, where she first heard of biochar—a term foreign to her ears but dripping with potential. The researchers spoke with a fervour that matched her own, their words painting pictures of soil stability and soil rejuvenation. This charcoal-like substance, when introduced to soil, held promises of improved structure, increased fertility, and form a bulwark against erosion. It whispered of a future where the land could stand its ground against the tempest's rage.

Maru's scepticism had been cautious, yet the data unfolded before her eyes like a rising dawn after a stormy night. Case studies showed lands restored, harvests multiplied. Real case studies, in Kenya. The investment made sense—the health of her soil was not just an environmental concern but a pact with prosperity, present and future. The thought of securing carbon credits was an engaging overture. If her adoption of biochar could fling open the gates to local wealth creation, what stood in the way?

Interaction with her soil was intimate, a dialogue of touch and response. As she spread the first of the biochar, her motions were deliberate, almost reverent. She envisaged the particles being mixed into the earth at the next ploughing, goodness seeping into the earth, a battalion of microscopic sentinels guarding against every drop that sought to wash the soil away, instead now channelling the water underground. Would the land remember this act of kindness? Would it reward her with abundance in the following seasons?

Maru's gaze fixed on the adjacent field, a canvas of green woven with the gold of ripening maize/corn, a small Eden where a biochar trial had already been embraced and was showing results. There was vitality present there—a testament as to what could be. Her mission was both simple and monumental—return what was taken from the earth, and the earth would return the favour a hundredfold.

As the sun began its descent, bathing the farm in amber light, Korie Maru imagined a time when the songs of her land would be taught to children not as a mournful ballad, but as an anthem of resurgence. With the close of the day came the promise of a new beginning, a possibility framed by the golden hues of hope. But as Maru watched the shadows stretch and grow, an unvoiced question lingered in the newfound silence—would the world realize the potential held in the black grains she cradled in her hands, or would they slip through humanity's fingers like the very soil they were meant to protect?

How Biochar is Revolutionizing Soil Preservation in Africa

The pivotal role of biochar in soil erosion prevention cannot be overstated, especially in regions prone to heavy rainfall or strong winds. In the battle against nature's forces, biochar emerges as a powerful ally, promoting soil structure improvement and reducing erosion to protect arable land. The implications of this go far beyond agriculture, offering a vital contribution to the preservation of natural resources and the maintenance of ecosystem integrity. In this chapter, we delve into the transformative impact of biochar in addressing soil erosion and its wide-ranging environmental benefits, underlining the crucial role it plays in unlocking Africa's green potential.

Understanding Biochar's Impact on Soil Structure and Erosion Reduction

Biochar's ability to enhance soil structure and reduce erosion is a game-changer, particularly in areas at risk of soil loss due to environmental factors. Biochar "breaks bulk and compaction" allowing water to penetrate deep into the soil, for future use by plants. By absorbing water and retaining nutrients, biochar has the potential to significantly reduce the impact of heavy rains, preventing soil runoff and preserving the vital topsoil layer which is normally washed away with the first heavy rains. In the face of strong winds, biochar acts as a stabilizing force, anchoring soil particles and mitigating erosion, thus safeguarding precious arable land from degradation. I have seen biochar also added on top of the soil to act as a mulch, creating a shaded cool micro-world full of microbial and insect activity at the surface of the soil.

Shaping a Resilient Environment and Agricultural System

Beyond its immediate impact on soil preservation, biochar contributes to broader environmental sustainability. By preventing soil loss and degradation, biochar protects the foundation of agriculture, ensuring the longevity of farming practices and the preservation of vital ecosystems. There is significant evidence that the bacteria and fungi housed in and on biochar actively metabolize and create fertility (explore 'Nitrogen Flush' if you want to dive in deep). In the African context, where agricultural activities are deeply intertwined with the natural environment, the role of biochar in fostering a resilient and sustainable agricultural system cannot be overstated.

Fostering Ecosystem Integrity and Agricultural Sustainability

The significance of biochar's contribution to ecosystem integrity and agricultural sustainability extends to the preservation of biodiversity and natural habitats. By maintaining soil fertility and integrity, biochar supports a harmonious coexistence between agricultural activities and local ecosystems. This not only safeguards the natural balance but also promotes the long-term sustainability of agricultural practices, fostering a holistic approach that benefits both the environment and local communities. A lot of agriculture in Africa is manual, and ½ acre to ¾ acre is the physical limit and provides sustenance for a family. By providing adequate food and productivity, the farmers are less prone to wander into a forested area, cut down the trees and farm there to take advantage of the fertile forest soils. Biochar prevents slash-and-burn farming.

Biochar's pivotal role in soil erosion prevention represents a transformative force in the quest for environmental sustainability and agricultural resilience. This chapter underscores the far-reaching implications of biochar, elevating it from a soil amendment to a catalyst for positive change in Africa and beyond. As we delve into the diverse applications of biochar, it becomes clear that its impact extends far beyond the soil, encompassing the broader ecosystem and the sustainable future of African agriculture.

In the pursuit of unlocking Africa's green potential, biochar emerges as a beacon of hope, offering practical and sustainable solutions to mitigate environmental challenges. By harnessing the potential of biochar, Africa has the opportunity to lead the way in sustainable agriculture, fostering a landscape of abundance, ecological harmony, and shared prosperity. The stakes are high, but the promise of a greener, more resilient future is within reach, and biochar stands at the forefront of this transformative journey. It is a simple win-win-win solution. The farmer wins. The investor wins. The global environment wins.

Soil erosion poses a significant threat to agricultural sustainability and ecosystem health, particularly in regions prone to heavy rains or wind. The erosion of fertile topsoil can lead to reduced crop yields, diminished land productivity, and the loss of essential nutrients. **This underscores the critical importance of understanding how biochar can improve soil structure and reduce erosion, especially in such vulnerable areas. There are many areas in Africa where the soi is now heavily dependent on artificially manufactured fertilizers, and their expense means low rates of**

application, with commensurately lower crop yields. This is further compounded by Forex losses against hard currencies, yet crops are sold in local currency. For example – UK's £ and Kenya's £ were at parity at independence, now 10:1. Meaning anything imported from UK is 1,000% more expensive. It is similar with the Euro and Dollar.

Through its ability to enhance soil structure, **biochar** plays a crucial role in preventing erosion. By promoting greater soil aggregation and enhancing water retention and groundwater penetration, biochar helps to stabilize the soil and reduces the risk of erosion caused by heavy rainfall or strong winds. This impact is particularly vital in regions such as Rift Valley and Kajiado, where bursts of heavy rains after drought can lead to devastating topsoil loss if not properly managed. **Biochar thus offers a compelling solution to combat the erosion of fertile soils essential for sustaining agriculture and local communities.**

Furthermore, biochar's porous structure provides a habitat for beneficial microorganisms such as bacteria, worms, micro-insects and fungi that contribute to soil health and resilience. Improved soil health directly correlates with reduced erosion, as the soil becomes better equipped to withstand the forces of nature. For small-scale farmers around Kisumu and Mombasa, where erosion due to heavy rainfall can threaten livelihoods, the integration of biochar into agricultural practices could be a game-changer, enhancing the long-term viability and productivity of their land.

The widespread application of biochar in areas like Nakuru and Thika has the potential to mitigate the detrimental effects of soil erosion, paving the way for sustainable agriculture and environmental preservation. By addressing the root causes of erosion, biochar holds the promise of safeguarding local ecosystems and ensuring the availability of fertile land for future generations.

Now, let's delve deeper into the broader environmental impact of biochar in preventing soil loss and preserving arable land...

Soil erosion is a critical environmental issue that threatens arable land and the stability of ecosystems. However, in the face of this challenge, biochar emerges as a powerful agent of change, offering a sustainable solution to prevent soil loss and preserve arable land. The broader environmental impact of biochar cannot be understated, especially in regions prone to heavy rains or wind. By exploring the multifaceted benefits of biochar, we can gain deeper insight into its potential to combat soil erosion and foster environmental sustainability.

Biochar, with its ability to improve soil structure and thus reduce erosion, plays a pivotal role in preventing soil loss and preserving arable land. This organic soil amendment tool not only mitigates the impact of heavy rains and wind but also enhances soil fertility and resilience. Through the retention of moisture and nutrients, **biochar** safeguards the integrity of the soil, thereby bolstering its capacity to support healthy plant growth and combat erosion.

In the broader context, the environmental impact of biochar extends far beyond individual farms and agricultural practices. By preventing soil loss and preserving arable land, biochar contributes to the preservation of natural resources and the maintenance of ecosystem integrity. Imagine the picturesque landscapes of the villages surrounding Nairobi or Nakuru, where the lush greenery of agricultural fields remains unmarred by erosion, thanks to the beneficial effects of biochar.

One cannot underestimate the profound impact of biochar on the overall health of an ecosystem, from the smallest microorganisms in the soil to the largest trees in the forest. By preserving arable land and preventing soil loss, **biochar** enables ecosystems to flourish, nurturing plant and animal life and creating a vibrant, sustainable environment within villages near urban centres like Mombasa and Kisumu.

Because CO_2 is a "common bad", the value of buried biochar reaches beyond the borders of Kenya, resonating globally in the context of carbon credits and the emerging green economy. The importance of soil conservation and sustainable agriculture is increasingly recognized, positioning biochar as an indispensable tool in the fight against climate change and environmental degradation. The **ethical and practical aspect of local wealth creation** through sustainable agricultural practices, enhanced by the use of biochar, exemplifies a model for global emulation, where value is created from the very lowest socio-economic levels of society, upwards. This is the opposite of "trickle-down economics – this is an economic upwelling".

In the grand tapestry of the global economy, the growing role of carbon credits as a means to incentivize sustainable practices underscores the significance of biochar in the prevention of soil erosion and preservation of arable land. With the potential to sequester carbon and mitigate greenhouse gas emissions, biochar embodies a tangible and impactful solution in the quest for environmental sustainability, echoing its benefits from Kenyan villages to international markets.

Biochar offers a sustainable solution that is pivotal to maintaining ecosystem integrity and enhancing agricultural sustainability. By harnessing the potential of biochar, we can champion the health of our planet and uplift communities at the same time. This powerful substance holds the key to transforming degraded soils into arable land, creating a flourishing environment for crops to thrive. Furthermore, by integrating biochar into agricultural practices, we can address the challenge of climate change by sequestering carbon and mitigating its impact on the environment.

Incorporating biochar into farming practices not only helps to preserve natural resources but also empowers local communities by promoting sustainable livelihoods from the ground up. Through proper implementation and widespread adoption of biochar, farmers can reduce the need for chemical fertilizers and promote organic, sustainable agricultural methods. Not only does this preserve soil health for future generations, but it also fosters a sense of environmental stewardship within communities.

Moreover, the global economy is increasingly recognizing the value of carbon credits as a means to combat climate change and encourage sustainable practices by acting as a channel to route financial payments from developed economies into farmers and communities in the third world directly. Biochar and the financial markets play a crucial role in this landscape, serving as a sustainable method for carbon sequestration. "Sustainability through profitability" is a self-serving, self-fulfilling prophecy. "Trade not Aid" is an oft-quoted maxim that is difficult to put into practice, not so with biochar projects. This directly correlates to the local wealth creation, and micro-macro scale FDI (Foreign Direct Investment), as communities can benefit from the economic opportunities tied to carbon credits. By selling carbon credits generated through the production of, and the soil-application of biochar to overseas and local investors, communities in Kenyan villages and beyond can secure a source of income that also contributes to positive environmental impact on a global scale. One tonne of biochar buried anywhere in the world, is three+ tonnes of CO_2 removed globally.

The promotion of biochar is not just about ecological sustainability, but also about creating a framework for lasting prosperity in local communities. By championing the widespread adoption of biochar, we can make a meaningful impact not only in preserving vital ecosystems but also in shaping a more ethical and practical future. This approach fosters a deep sense of local wealth creation, community involvement, local ownership and ensures that the benefits of harnessing biochar are harvested by the communities who steward the lands. In doing so, we can empower local communities to take an active role in preserving the environment while also improving their economic stability.

By embracing the potential of biochar, we can forge a path towards a future where human actions work in harmony with nature, rather than against it. The role of biochar in maintaining ecosystem integrity and promoting agricultural sustainability is not just a scientific breakthrough; it's a testament to the power of innovation in transforming our relationship with our environment. Through its promotion and widespread adoption, we can bring about meaningful change in communities and ecosystems, uplifting the planet and its people simultaneously.

In embracing **biochar** as a pivotal tool in the fight against soil erosion, we are not just addressing a localized issue (reduced crop yields due to soil infertility); we are championing a cause that holds the key to the preservation of natural resources and the sustainability of agricultural practices around the globe. By harnessing the power of **biochar** to improve soil structure and reduce erosion, especially in regions around Kisumu and Mombasa where heavy rains and wind pose significant challenges, we are contributing to a worldwide effort to maintain the integrity of ecosystems. This shift towards sustainable agricultural practices has far-reaching implications, not just for the local communities in Kenya but for the global economy as well. I will not dwell on "illegal immigration and waves of immigrants" – but well-fed employed farmer-people do not undertake perilous voyages across oceans in small flimsy boats.

The impact of **biochar** cannot be understated. Through its ability to prevent soil loss and preserve arable land, it is shaping the landscape of environmental conservation and agricultural sustainability. From the bustling market farms around Nairobi to the tranquil surroundings of Eldama Ravine, the role of **biochar** in promoting these critical ecological and agricultural changes cannot be overlooked. It is not merely a local solution; it is a global asset in our efforts to combat the challenges of climate change and ecosystem degradation. It is only right that people in the third world can sell their carbon credits to companies that need to offset their CO_2 emissions, be it a mega corporation like Microsoft, or a household in Oregon with a business traveller family member.

As we continue to delve into the potential of **biochar** in soil erosion prevention, it is vital to recognize the practical and ethical implications of local wealth creation. The implementation of **biochar** systems presents an opportunity for the most marginalized and deprived Kenyan communities to cultivate economic prosperity through sustainable practices. Simultaneously, it addresses the urgent need for environmental preservation, and a side-benefactor will be Mother Nature, and increased biodiversity. This fusion of practicality and ethics creates a framework for change that transcends boundaries, uplifting communities while safeguarding our planet.

The emergence of carbon credits in the global economy further underscores the relevance of **biochar** in sustainability efforts. Around cities from Kisumu to Mombasa, the potential for generating carbon credits through **biochar** projects holds the promise of economic rejuvenation in rural communities. These credits not only incentivize environmentally friendly practices but also empower local communities to drive positive change while reaping the benefits of their work directly.

In realizing the potential of **biochar** in soil erosion prevention, in mineral retention, we are not simply employing a farming technique, we are igniting a movement. It is a movement that embodies hope, resilience, and a commitment to safeguarding our planet. It is a movement that transcends borders, incorporating ethical practices and practical solutions. As we forge ahead in this revolution, let us stand united in our dedication to leveraging the power of **biochar** for the betterment of our world.

Chapter 4: Biochar's Contribution to Water Conservation

It was a crisp morning in the hills overlooking Nairobi, the sunlight dancing on the rusted roofs like a capricious sprite, casting shadows that moved to the rhythm of a distant city waking up. Wangui Wambui stood in her modest yard, feet sinking into the soft earth, hands on her hips, surveying her small parcel of land with a blend of determination and worry. Here, where the rain was as unpredictable as a coin toss, her dreams of a lush vegetable garden were often scorched by the relentless sun before they could take root.

Wangui had learned of biochar from a local workshop, touted as the hidden jewel that could turn barren soils into fertile grounds. The high porosity of this charred organic matter could help the earth retain water, and in her drought-prone region, this was not just a convenience, it was the difference between plenty and want. She remembered the instructor's words, "With biochar, Wangui, your land will drink and hold onto the rain, making every drop count."

A breeze whispered through the neighbour's maize, rustling like a secret being passed from one leaf to another. She reached down, let her fingers graze the cool, dark substance she had mixed into the soil. The biochar felt like hope, gritty and substantial. Her thoughts turned to the reservoir of water it could help her soil retain, reducing the need for frequent irrigation, conserving that precious resource.

Fire To Life

"Could this be the solution we have been praying for?" she mused, as a bulbul bird trilled a tentative daybreak hymn. She much preferred bulbuls to mousebirds, which were essentially winged rats and destructive.

She thought of her fellow farmers, their foreheads creased with the familiar etchings of anxiety, their backs bent, not in humble toil but under the weight of uncertainty. "How many more would need to know of this, to believe in the revival of their farms?" pondered Wangui. She envisaged gatherings under the mugumo trees, traditionally revered as sacred by her tribe, the trainings imparting the wisdom of sustainable water management, of resilience against the creeping dread of climate change which had devastated the last three years of crops. Longer droughts are now commonplace in Kenya and several other countries in Africa.

In the distance, children laughed on their way to school, their voices lifting the corners of Wangui's mouth into a smile. She permitted herself a moment's fantasy – her garden thriving, children fed, the community united. Beyond the borders of her farm, she saw her action as a pebble in a pond, the ripples turning into waves of change, whispering of carbon credits, a wealth that could be cultivated and shared.

Wangui's musings were interrupted by the cheery voice of her neighbour, calling out a greeting over the fence. "Eh, Wangui, what's this black gold you're mixing into the land?" His curiosity was matched by his scepticism.

"This," she said, turning towards him, a zealous glint in her eye, "is the future of our farms." She beckoned him over, ready to share her discovery, to weave another thread into the fabric of a community poised for transformation.

As she shared her insight with her neighbour, showing him the granules of potential, she wondered just how far the tendrils of change could stretch. Would the whole of Kenya, even, understand that this was more than cultivation? It was creation – of wealth, of food security, of life – in the face of adversity. Could Kenya pioneer a movement, she wondered, where the soil speaks of endurance and ingenuity?

How many more Wangui Wambuis, with hands toiled in biochar and hearts ablaze with hope, would it take to turn the tides of climate and scarcity?

Unveiling Biochar's Power in Water Conservation

With approximately 75% of the land in Africa classified as arid or semi-arid, water scarcity presents a significant challenge to sustainable agriculture. In this pivotal chapter, we delve into the remarkable potential of biochar in revolutionizing water conservation practices, particularly in drought-prone regions.

Biochar's high porosity offers a game-changing solution to the pressing issue of water penetration into and retention in soils, underlining the crucial role it plays in promoting sustainable water management and reducing water usage in agriculture. Furthermore, biochar emerges as a resilient ally in mitigating the adverse impacts of climate change on water resources, unlocking a new era of environmental sustainability and agricultural productivity.

After drought, the topsoil gets baked hard in the African sun, especially areas that are overgrazed. When it finally rains, the water just rushes off, carrying the topsoil with it. The high porosity of biochar creates small holes, loosening the soil, allowing the first rains to soak into the ground. This allows it to act as a sponge in the soil, **retaining water** and reducing the risk of runoff during heavy rainfall or irrigation. This not only ensures a more efficient use of water but also mitigates soil erosion, safeguarding vital nutrients and preventing sedimentation in water bodies and subsequently river banks overflowing. By fostering this water retention capability, biochar becomes an indispensable tool in combatting the challenges posed by unpredictable rainfall patterns and prolonged droughts, offering a lifeline to agricultural communities across Kenya, from Kisumu to Nairobi to Mombasa.

As we scrutinize the potential of biochar in promoting sustainable water management, a fundamental truth emerges: biochar empowers farmers to adopt **resilient agricultural practices**. By reducing the frequency of irrigation and enhancing the soil's ability to retain moisture, biochar not only conserves water but also cultivates an environment conducive to improved crop yields. This dual benefit underscores the profound impact of biochar in building climate-resilient agricultural systems that can withstand the rigors of a changing climate. Imagine the transformation of rural landscapes around Kisumu, as biochar-infused soils yield bountiful harvests while conserving precious water resources and retaining minerals and nutrients.

The climate crisis looms large over the global community, affecting water resources and agricultural productivity alike. Here, biochar emerges as a beacon of hope, offering a tangible solution to mitigate the **impacts of climate change** on water resources. As extreme weather events become more frequent, and droughts longer and more severe, the role of biochar in preserving water becomes an essential element of sustainable development. From Eldoret to Nakuru, the integration of biochar into agricultural landscapes paints a vivid picture of resilient communities adapting to the challenges of a changing climate and embracing a sustainable future.

The synthesis of biochar and water conservation transcends mere agricultural innovation; it symbolizes a paradigm shift towards a more sustainable and environmentally conscious future. By reducing water usage, supporting resilient agricultural practices, and fortifying the resilience of water resources, biochar stands as a powerful agent of change. It offers a blueprint for the sustainable management of one of Africa's most precious resources—water. Nairobi, with its bustling urban centre, and the rural heartlands of Kenya alike, stand to benefit from the transformative potential of biochar, ushering in a new era of environmental stewardship and agricultural prosperity. Underground water tables will rise as more water percolates underground. We will not delve too much into the reduction of nitrates leaching into ground water if biochar is mixed into the soil, nor point out that most domestic water filter jugs and filter systems consist of little more than activated charcoal in a filter medium.

In the next section, we'll delve deeper into the practical applications of biochar in water conservation, exploring case studies and real-world examples that showcase the tangible impact of this revolutionary approach. Together, we will unravel the full extent of biochar's potential and its unparalleled capacity to unlock Africa's green potential, one sustainable droplet at a time.

Biochar's high porosity and water retention capacity is a game-changer for addressing water scarcity in drought-prone regions. The remarkable capacity of biochar to retain water in the soil offers a lifeline to communities grappling with dwindling water resources. By making biochar swales, ditches and other structures to trap water, we will reverse the dramatic decline of Kenya's underground water table. (I think the officer from Nema I spoke to said it is dropping 5 metres per year in Nairobi where boreholes regularly run dry and have to be re-drilled deeper) Think about the impact this could have in big cities like Nairobi and Mombasa, and even more so – smaller towns and villages where access to clean water is a daily struggle for many. It is not a cliché, rather a sad reality that a number of African women and girls walk several kilometres daily to go fetch household water. By incorporating biochar into agricultural practices, the cycle of water scarcity can be broken, raising groundwater tables and thus empowering farmers and communities to build resilience in the face of climate change challenges.

The water-retention properties of biochar are a revelation for regions like Kenya, where erratic rainfall patterns have become the norm and groundwater tables are falling with boreholes drying up regularly. **Soils enriched with biochar have displayed significantly improved water-penetration and holding capacity, reducing the need for frequent irrigation and easing the burden on strained water supplies.** Imagine the transformation in areas like Mombasa, where water is piped in from Mzima Springs about 200Km away. Agriculture often contends with chronic water shortages, with reports of 40-year-old mango trees and cashew nut trees dying in 2023 due to drought. With biochar, not only can the resilience of crops be bolstered, but water conservation becomes a reality, fostering sustainable agricultural practices in the long run.

As we fast-forward to envision the impact of biochar on water conservation, we may see village landscapes outside Kisumu thriving with well-nourished soils, enriched with the liquid gold of biochar, rather than the striga-weed infested farms we see currently, a sign that they are lacking in fertility. By significantly reducing water usage in agriculture, biochar can contribute to the alleviation of water stress in urban and peri-urban areas. The implications extend beyond immediate relief in raising water tables and laying the groundwork for long-term sustainability in water management.

The implications of high porosity and water-holding capacity in biochar embody a hope for communities facing water scarcity, offering a path towards lasting change. As we consider the potential impact of biochar's water retention capabilities, it's easy to imagine the transformation it could bring to communities across Kenya and other African countries. The use of biochar in agriculture becomes an avenue for environmental sustainability and local wealth creation, fostering a profound shift towards resilience in the face of water scarcity. **The opportunity to transform water management and agricultural practices through biochar is nothing short of revolutionary, promising a future where the impact of droughts and water scarcity can be mitigated.**

Exploring this potential further, let's delve into the role of biochar in promoting sustainable water management and its contribution to mitigating the impacts of climate change on water resources.

In the context of water scarcity, **biochar** emerges as a game-changer, offering a sustainable solution for water management and the mitigation of climate change impacts on water resources. While the challenges posed by water scarcity may appear daunting, biochar presents an opportunity to address this issue with lasting impact. In Kenyan villages, rural communities and beyond, the application of biochar holds promise for transforming agricultural practices and fostering sustainable water management, delivering positive outcomes for ecosystems, biodiversity and communities. By harnessing the high porosity of biochar to channel water underground and retain water in soils, we can create a ripple effect that strengthens the resilience of water-stressed regions, paving the way for a more sustainable future.

The role of biochar in **promoting sustainable water management** is closely intertwined with the tangible benefits it offers. Water conservation becomes a reality when we recognize the potential of biochar to optimize water usage in agricultural settings, leading to improved soil moisture penetration and retention. The deployment of biochar in Kenyan villages and farming communities can catalyse a shift towards eco-friendly farming practices, minimizing water wastage and enhancing the efficiency of irrigation systems. Furthermore, this sustainable approach to water management aligns with the growing emphasis on environmental consciousness and improving soil fertility thus positioning biochar as a crucial player in the global push for resource sustainability.

In light of **mitigating the impacts of climate change on water resources**, biochar serves as a powerful ally in fortifying ecosystems against the destabilizing effects of a changing climate. By integrating biochar into soil management practices, we have the potential to mitigate the risks associated with erratic rainfall patterns, thereby safeguarding water resources for future generations. This approach is not just relevant in Kenyan rural communities , but globally, as sustainability, regenerative agriculture and food security has become an increasingly urgent global need. The emphasis on resilience in the face of climate change is at the core of biochar's mission, making it an essential component in adapting to and mitigating the effects of environmental change.

While the intricacies of **sustainable water management** and the **mitigation of climate change impacts** pose complex challenges, biochar offers practical and actionable solutions, presenting a beacon of hope for communities facing water scarcity. The application of biochar brings forth a narrative of empowerment, enabling local farmers and communities in Kenyan villages and smaller towns to cultivate a more sustainable, water-conscious approach to agriculture. By embracing biochar, communities can reclaim control over their water resources, carving out a path to resilience and sustainability in the face of environmental adversity.

As we look towards the future, the growing role of **carbon credits** in the global economy cannot be overlooked as a major financial incentivising mechanism. Biochar's potential to sequester carbon and mitigate greenhouse gas emissions (both CO_2 and Methane) aligns closely with the world's momentum towards carbon neutrality and sustainable development. Implementing biochar burial as a strategy for sustainable water management opens up new avenues for local wealth creation, creating a beneficial cycle that not only uplifts communities but also contributes to global environmental goals. By empowering local communities to participate in carbon credit programs, the ethical and practical aspect of wealth creation intersects, fostering a sense of shared responsibility for environmental stewardship.

In Kenya and beyond, the inclusion of biochar burial in sustainable water management systems represents an opportunity to amplify the impact of environmental stewardship. Through the strategic deployment of biochar, communities can transcend water scarcity, cultivating a future defined by resilience, sustainability, and collective wealth creation. As the global community continues its quest for sustainable solutions, the virtues of biochar stand tall, offering a transformative pathway towards a more eco-conscious and water-secure future.

Understanding the Role of Biochar in Reducing Water Usage and Supporting Resilient Agricultural Practices

In the pursuit of **sustainable agricultural practices and water conservation**, biochar stands out as a remarkable solution. This framework will provide a comprehensive overview of the different applications of biochar in agriculture, shedding light on how this "liquid magnet" can drastically reduce water usage and support resilient agricultural practices. Let's explore the key components of this framework and how they contribute to its overall function.

Soil Amendment:

Biochar acts as a soil conditioner, enhancing soil structure, pH and boosting its water retention capacity. Its high porosity allows it to absorb and retain water, providing a reservoir for plants during dry periods. Moreover, biochar fosters the growth of beneficial microorganisms micro-insects and fungi in the soil, further contributing to its water-holding capacity. When integrated into agricultural practices, biochar significantly reduces water usage by ensuring that the soil remains adequately hydrated for plant growth.

Livestock Feed Supplement:

When used as a feed supplement for livestock, biochar offers unique benefits. There is evidence it aids in improving the digestion process in animals, leading to reduced methane production in the order of

10% for livestock like cattle. Moreover, by enhancing the nutrient retention and metabolism of chickens, biochar directly contributes to improved growth, In Kenya it is common to see chickens pecking at and eating small bits of charcoal.

Crop Protection Method:

Biochar's ability to suppress certain soil-borne pathogens provides a valuable avenue for crop protection. By reducing the prevalence of diseases in crops, biochar indirectly supports resilient agricultural practices. Healthy crops are more efficient in their water usage, as they are better equipped to utilize the available water for growth and development.

These components of the framework are interconnected, each playing a critical role in reducing water usage and fostering resilient agriculture. The dynamics of the framework are influenced by the balance and interaction of these components, creating a sustainable ecosystem within agricultural practices.

The practical implications of this framework are profound. By integrating biochar into agriculture, we are not only reducing water usage but also embracing a regenerative approach that promotes sustainable land management. This approach not only leads to enhanced soil fertility but also sets the stage for long-term climate change mitigation.

Fire To Life

In Kenya, where increasing water scarcity is a pressing concern, the role of biochar in reducing water usage and supporting resilient agricultural practices is of paramount importance. As the global economy increasingly recognizes the value of carbon credits, the local adoption of biochar can potentially be linked to carbon credit initiatives, ensuring that local wealth creation aligns with ethical and sustainable practices. This creates a powerful narrative of environmental stewardship coupled with economic growth, positioning Kenya at the forefront of sustainable agricultural practices.

Joining the biochar revolution isn't just a choice; it's a commitment to a greener future—a future where significant water conservation, soil regeneration and resilient agricultural practices become the norm. In this journey, each step towards embracing biochar contributes to the ecosystem's well-being and uplifts communities financially, paving the way for a brighter, sustainable tomorrow.

In harnessing the potential of biochar, we stand at the forefront of a watershed moment for water conservation in Kenya and beyond. The high porosity of biochar presents a game-changing opportunity to address water scarcity, particularly in drought-prone regions like Narok, Kajiado and Machakos. By enhancing soil water retention and improving soil fertility, biochar not only supports agriculture but also mitigates the impacts of climate change on water resources, a key concern in rural communities. This simple yet profound solution holds the power to revolutionize our approach to water management, setting the stage for a more sustainable and resilient future.

As we look to the future, it's crucial to recognize the pivotal role of biochar in supporting local communities while contributing to the global economy through the growing prominence of carbon credits. This presents an ethical and practical opportunity for wealth creation at the local level, empowering farming communities in places like Eldoret and Nakuru (two of Kenya's largest agricultural towns) to thrive sustainably. The potential for biochar to reduce water usage and bolster resilient agricultural practices is not just a theoretical concept; it is a tangible avenue for positive change that can uplift ecosystems and communities alike.

The time has come to embrace biochar as a catalyst for sustainable water management, paving the way for a future where water scarcity is but a distant memory. Through our collective effort and commitment to leveraging biochar's potential, we have the chance to create lasting impact, not only in our local communities but also on a global scale. Let us move forward with an unwavering resolve to integrate biochar into our sustainable water and soil management strategies, ensuring a future where the scarcity of water is a challenge long surpassed, and where thriving ecosystems and communities abound.

Chapter 5: Biochar for Sustainable Waste Management

Under the Kenyan sun, in the bustling city of Kisumu, Akinyi Onyango mulled over the vast stretches of sugarcane plantations dotting the landscape beyond the outskirts of the city. Each year, these fields amassed thousands of tonnes of agricultural waste, an enduring dilemma for the local farmers and an ecological conundrum for Akinyi, an earnest environmental engineer. She'd envisioned a transition for Kisumu's bagasse mountains, a paradigm shift from mere waste to wealth, and biochar was the key that could unlock this potential.

With each step she took on the sun-baked street, her thoughts mirrored the rhythmic tapping of her shoes on the concrete pavement. Akinyi had once read about the Amazonian Terra Preta, the pre-Columbian black earth, imbued with biochar thousands of years ago, and she envisioned recreating such fertile ground on Kenyan soil. The air smelled of heat and industry, like rain on hot tar, a scent that fuelled her aspirations for change.

She observed the city's heartbeat, the hawkers calling, buses roaring, and amidst it, the occasional tree standing defiant against the urban sprawl. They spoke to Akinyi of resilience and balance, and she knew the implementation of biochar technology could reinforce that harmony. The conversion of agricultural by-products and food waste into a carbon-rich amendment that could rejuvenate the countryside's green farming spaces and boost peri-urban agriculture enthralled her.

However, it was not just the soil's fertility that concerned her; Akinyi saw biochar's role through a broader scope. It could help abate the greenhouse gases that were birthed from the organic waste rotting in landfills and actively combat climate change, especially methane, said to be 30 to 80 times more damaging than CO_2—a formidable foe that spared no corner of the globe. It dawned on her that Kenya's agricultural towns and cities could not only reduce their carbon footprints but also tap into the burgeoning carbon credit market. This initiative could weave wealth into the community's fabric, transforming environmental stewardship into tangible welfare.

At a quaint roadside café, where the clinking of dishes punctuated the hum of conversation, Akinyi discussed her proposal with Omondi, an enthusiastic young farmer who shared her vision. They spoke of crop yields, of hardy maize and vibrant vegetables bolstered by charcoal-infused soil. The potential for local wealth creation through sustainable, ethical means was palpable in their exchange. It was no longer just a concept but a possible reality, speaking to the optimism that Kisumu and its surrounding people carried within.

As the sun began its descent, casting the city in an amber glow, the imperative became clearer to Akinyi. The practicality of biochar as a keystone for the circular economy, the ethical component that cradled local prosperity—these were the transformative forces she was poised to harness for her community and environment. But the question lingered, as it often did at the crossroads of innovation and tradition: Would the rest of the city recognize the value in her plan, and join in transforming waste into a wellspring of life for Kisumu then the rest of the cities in Kenya?

Harnessing Biochar for Sustainable Waste Management

In the quest for sustainable waste management and environmental conservation, the potential of biochar cannot be overstated. Chapter 5 delves into the transformative power of biochar in converting agricultural and organic waste into a valuable resource, presenting an innovative solution to the detrimental environmental impact of waste decomposition. This insight opens up a new frontier in curbing greenhouse gas emissions (both methane and CO_2), promoting circular economy principles, and championing the responsible management of organic waste.

In the heart of the African continent, where agricultural activities thrive, the abundance of agricultural waste material provides a unique opportunity. This chapter sheds light on how African farmers, entrepreneurs, and individuals can leverage biochar production to not only address waste management challenges but also contribute to environmental sustainability. By recognizing the potential of biochar and understanding its role in minimizing the environmental impact of waste decomposition, a profound shift towards a greener, more conscientious approach to waste management takes place.

The process outlined in Chapter 5 is designed to empower individuals to convert agricultural waste materials into biochar with ease and efficiency. This process is accessible to farmers and anyone interested in participating in the sustainable management of organic waste. By following the guidelines set forth in this chapter, individuals can actively contribute to environmental sustainability by harnessing biochar from agricultural waste materials, thus unlocking Africa's green potential in an impactful and tangible manner.

The process for producing biochar from agricultural waste materials is the cornerstone of this chapter. Starting with the collection of agricultural and food waste, the process guides individuals through the preparation and carbonization of the feedstock, right through to the utilization or commercialization of the produced biochar. This holistic approach ensures that every phase of the process is actionable, impactful, and in alignment with the overarching goal of sustainable environmental stewardship.

The objective of this process is crystal clear: to convert agricultural and food waste materials into biochar, thus promoting sustainable waste management and environmental conservation. With each step logically leading to the next, the process provides a manageable, achievable pathway for individuals to actively contribute to a circular economy and minimize their environmental footprint. Evaluation and feedback mechanisms within the process ensure that individuals can continuously improve and refine their biochar production efforts, driving towards greater efficacy and impact.

Throughout this process, flexibility and feedback is not only allowed but encouraged to allow for iterative adjustments. The practical considerations of various environments, waste materials, and production capacities demand adaptability, ensuring that individuals can tailor the process to their specific context. The inclusion of a timeframe and defined completion criteria instils a sense of purpose and momentum, ensuring that the process moves forward with a clear direction and measurable outcomes.

Harnessing biochar for sustainable waste management is a tangible way for individuals to contribute to a greener, more resilient future. By following the step-by-step process meticulously laid out in Chapter 5, individuals can navigate the transformative journey of turning agricultural waste materials into biochar, creating local wealth from waste and making a meaningful impact on the global environmental landscape.

The potential of biochar production to transform waste into wealth is not a distant concept but a palpable reality, ready to be embraced and harnessed by individuals eager to make a positive difference.

Biochar presents a remarkable opportunity to transform agricultural and organic waste into a valuable resource, addressing waste management challenges and promoting environmental sustainability. The process of converting this waste into biochar not only reduces the environmental impact of waste decomposition but also offers a solution to the global challenge of waste management. Harnessing biochar for sustainable waste management can lead to the creation of circular economy principles and minimize greenhouse gas emissions. This valuable resource has the potential to play a significant role in elevating the environmental and economic landscape of communities, particularly in Kenyan communities and towns.

The conversion of organic waste into biochar is a promising venture that offers a plethora of environmental and economic benefits. **By converting agricultural and other organic waste into biochar, we can greatly reduce carbon emissions while creating a valuable byproduct.** This process can bring about substantial improvements in waste management practices and contribute to mitigating climate change. Some may overlook organic and food waste as a problem, but the truth is that it presents an opportunity for valuable transformation.

Fire To Life

The valuable resource that biochar offers is not just limited to environmental impact. The potential for wealth creation through biochar production is significant. In Kenyan towns and cities, where waste management is a persistent challenge, the creation of biochar from agricultural and organic waste opens up avenues for local wealth creation. *Harnessing biochar presents the opportunity to not only mitigate environmental impact but also create economic opportunities within local communities.*

Kenyan cities, like many urban centres across the globe, are experiencing an increasing demand for sustainable waste management solutions. Harnessing biochar for sustainable waste management can serve as a model for enhancing organic waste management practices, leading to a cleaner and more sustainable environment. The production of biochar from agricultural and organic waste has the potential to revolutionize how these wastes are managed within urban settings. This presents a compelling prospect for transforming waste management practices on a global scale, where sustainable solutions are greatly needed.

The noteworthy contribution of biochar to sustainable waste management cannot be overemphasized. It is an opportunity to address the environmental challenges associated with waste management, offering a viable and eco-friendly alternative. The process of converting agricultural and organic waste into biochar not only curbs greenhouse gas emissions but also presents a practical and ethical means of local wealth creation. This dual impact speaks to the potential of biochar to transform waste into a valuable resource, providing a powerful example of the circular economy paradigm in action.

Embracing the potential of biochar in sustainable waste management opens the door to a world of environmental and economic possibilities. Let's explore the far-reaching impacts and opportunities that this process presents.

Biochar presents an incredible opportunity to support more sustainable waste management practices by converting agricultural and organic waste into a valuable resource. This transformational process not only offers a solution to the challenge of organic waste management but also has the potential to curb greenhouse gas emissions and promote circular economy principles. By harnessing the power of biochar, we can revolutionize the way we view waste, turning what was once considered a problem into a valuable asset for our communities and the environment.

In rural communities, towns and cities like Kisumu, Nairobi and Mombasa, where agricultural, food and organic waste can pose significant disposal challenges, biochar production offers a promising solution. By converting this waste into biochar, we can mitigate the harmful impact of waste decomposition on local ecosystems and the atmosphere, ultimately contributing to a greener, cleaner environment for all. Additionally, in the context of the broader global economy, the growing role of carbon credits offers an exciting avenue for communities to benefit financially from their biochar production, further emphasizing the ethical and practical aspect of local wealth creation.

The potential of biochar in curbing greenhouse gas emissions cannot be overstated. By converting organic waste into biochar, we can effectively sequester carbon, preventing it from being released into the atmosphere as greenhouse gases. This process not only reduces the environmental impact of waste but also contributes to mitigating climate change, nurturing a healthier future for our planet. As we work to promote circular economy principles, biochar production stands out as a beacon of innovation and sustainability, showcasing the transformative power of harnessing waste for the greater good.

Utilizing biochar to address waste management challenges has far-reaching implications, both locally and globally. The creation of biochar from organic waste presents not only an eco-friendly solution to waste management but also an opportunity for communities to participate in sustainable economic practices that have positive, lasting effects. In Kenyan cities, this translates to tangible benefits for individuals and neighbourhoods, fostering a sense of community pride and contributing to the collective effort to build a more environmentally conscious society.

As we continue to explore the potential of biochar, it is important to recognize the profound impact it can have on local communities and the broader global landscape. The ethical and practical aspects of local wealth creation through biochar production offer a powerful incentive for communities to engage in sustainable waste management practices. By embracing the use of biochar, communities can not only reduce waste and curb greenhouse gas emissions but also actively participate in building a more sustainable future for generations to come.

In a world where environmental responsibility is increasingly crucial, the role of biochar in curbing greenhouse gas emissions and promoting circular economy principles cannot be overlooked. By championing the transformative power of biochar, we can set a new standard for waste management, uplifting communities and nurturing ecosystems with a fervour that echoes far beyond our immediate surroundings. Through collective action and a commitment to sustainable practices, the potential of biochar to navigate towards a future of environmental resilience and abundance is within reach.

The role of biochar in minimizing the environmental impact of organic waste decomposition is a crucial aspect of sustainable waste management. By converting agricultural and organic waste into a valuable resource, biochar plays a significant role in curbing greenhouse gas emissions and promoting circular economy principles. This process not only addresses waste management challenges but also minimizes the environmental impact of waste decomposition, particularly in urban areas like Kisumu, Nairobi and Mombasa, where organic waste poses a significant environmental challenge.

In Kenya's urban centres, a staggering amount of organic and food waste is generated daily, straining the existing waste management infrastructure. The decomposition of this organic waste releases harmful greenhouse gases (methane and CO_2) into the atmosphere, contributing to climate change and local environmental degradation. Here, the innovative use of biochar presents an exciting opportunity to mitigate these challenges. By converting organic waste into biochar, not only can the harmful emissions be reduced, but a valuable resource and value-creating economic resource can be created in the process.

The emphasis on local wealth creation through the production of biochar cannot be overstated. In cities like Kisumu Nakuru and Eldoret, where communities are seeking viable economic opportunities, the production of biochar from organic food waste can create employment and entrepreneurial ventures. Additionally, the resulting biochar can be utilized to enrich soils in these agricultural centres, promoting sustainable agriculture and enhancing food security in local communities. Here lies a chance for communities to not only address waste management challenges but also make a positive impact on their local economy and environment.

Furthermore, the global economy is increasingly recognizing the significance of carbon credits. This incentive for reducing emissions and sequestering carbon presents an exciting opportunity, particularly for emerging economies like Kenya. The production of biochar from organic waste offers the potential for communities to access and benefit from these carbon markets, further incentivizing sustainable waste management practices and the creation of local wealth through financial markets.

As we delve into understanding the role of biochar in minimizing the environmental impact of organic waste decomposition, it becomes evident that the potential for positive change is substantial. The transformative impact reaches beyond waste management, offering opportunities for wealth creation, environmental protection, and participation in the global carbon credit economy. This innovative approach holds the promise of a brighter, more sustainable future for communities in Kenya and beyond. The transition from waste to wealth through biochar production promises to uplift ecosystems, empower communities, and contribute to a more sustainable and prosperous future.

The potential of biochar in waste management cannot be overstated. It offers a transformative solution to the seemingly insurmountable challenge of agricultural and organic waste disposal, presenting an opportunity to convert these waste streams into valuable resources with myriad environmental benefits. **Through the harnessing of biochar, we have the means to not only address waste management challenges but also to significantly reduce greenhouse gas emissions in our communities.**

As we delve into the realm of waste management, it becomes evident that biochar is a beacon of hope, shining a light on the path towards a sustainable future by reducing CO2 and methane emissions. By adopting biochar production, individuals and communities can seize the opportunity to create wealth from what was once considered waste. This embodies the spirit of the circular economy, where every resource, no matter how humble its origins, has the potential to be transformed into something valuable and used to enrich agricultural soil. **This presents an ethical and practical pathway to local wealth creation, displaying the intrinsic value of repurposing organic waste streams for the benefit of the rural community and the world at large.**

Moreover, as the world increasingly recognizes the urgency of mitigating climate change, biochar emerges as a pivotal player in the global economy. The rise of carbon credits as a means to reduce greenhouse gas emissions places biochar at the forefront of sustainable initiatives. By curbing emissions through the conversion of waste into biochar, communities not only contribute to the preservation of the environment but also stand to benefit from this virtuous cycle of waste conversion. **The evolving role of carbon credits in the global economy reinforces the attractiveness of harnessing biochar for sustainable waste management, offering a twofold incentive for communities to embrace this innovative approach.**

In recognizing the enormity of the opportunity that biochar offers, it becomes clear that the shift from waste to wealth is well within reach. This transformative process not only offers a solution to the challenges of waste management and greenhouse gas emissions but also embodies the ethos of sustainability and prosperity for communities across Kenya and beyond. **The journey from waste to wealth through biochar is a testament to our ability to create meaningful change and steward our planet toward a greener, more prosperous future.**

Chapter 6: Biochar's Impact on Biodiversity

Amidst the hustle and bustle of Nairobi's morning, with the sun just cresting over the horizon and casting a golden hue upon the awakening city, a middle-aged Kenyan farmer named Thiong'o had just delivered his kales at the market and strolled through the streets to get back to his modest plot of land about 40km away. He was amongst a community of market garden farmers that grew fresh greens for the city's populace. Back on his farm, he felt the damp earth had changed beneath his gumboots, a softness now crunchy and noisier, heralded by the recent application of biochar. The once-barren soil now clutched the promise of fertility in its newly-darkened embrace.

Thiong'o's brow furrowed as he surveyed his farm, recalling how his grandfather had taught him about the importance of working the land responsibly. He thought about the connection, as ancient as the few remaining acacia trees, between the health of the soil and the splendour of life it could sustain. The introduction of biochar, this charcoal-like substance he'd only learned about at a local agronomy workshop, was his testament to that ancestral wisdom.

He observed the new shoots of maize reaching for the sky, alongside the kale and pigeon peas that seemed to thrive in the biochar-amended soil. The previous years had been hard, with infertile soil, low rains and pest invasions. But Thiong'o clung to the hope that a change was on the horizon. Biodiversity had been a fading tale in these parts, yet with biochar, the winds whispered possibilities of its return.

Interactions interrupted his reverie as he dug a small patch—a small assembly of earthworms writhing jubilantly through the soil, a vivid testament to the soil's newfound vitality. Kibet knew their renewed presence after decades meant more than just healthy soil; it meant birds would follow, and a cascade of life would spring forth from this rejuvenated foundation.

As he ran his hands through a pile of biochar, the soot marking his skin, he contemplated the carbon credits his new farming practices might earn. An ethical win that also meant local wealth creation, aligning with his dreams of better education for his children, and perhaps an ease to the tightness that often gripped his chest when bills were due.

Nearby, children played, their laughter piercing the ambient sounds of the city in the distance, reminding him that the future was more than just crops—it was about nurturing life in all its forms, ensuring the resilience of ecosystems upon which his community depended.

Thiong'o was no scientist, but the earth spoke to him, told him of the microscopic communities flourishing in the roots and of the return of insects not seen in years. He was becoming a guardian of a tiny Eden within the vastness of Limuru, on the outskirts of Nairobi, an Eden that humbly resisted the encroaching concrete with every sprout, every bloom.

As the day progressed and he walked back home, he pondered the profound yet simple acts of adding biochar to soil, a decision that ripples outward, affecting countless lives, especially if his neighbours followed his example. Could this simple substance truly hold the key to rebirth for all the local ecosystems on the brink? Could it, and the actions of humble farmers like Thiong'o, stand as a bulwark against the tide of soil-degradation? And if so, what transformations would the coming seasons unveil under the nurturing sun of Kenya?

Unlocking Nature's Potential: Biochar's Impact on Biodiversity

The interconnectedness of healthier soils, greater biodiversity, and biochar's role in supporting robust ecosystems is a pivotal focus in understanding the broader ecological impact of biochar. This insight underscores the potential of biochar to nurture diverse habitats and promote the resilience of natural ecosystems, aligning perfectly with the overarching goal of environmental conservation. In this chapter, we delve into the intricate web of relationships between biochar, biodiversity, and environmental sustainability. By examining biochar's contribution to maintaining healthy, diverse habitats and promoting the resilience of natural ecosystems, we gain a deeper understanding of how biochar fosters biodiversity, paving the way for the preservation of our environment.

By promoting habitat diversity and ecosystem resilience, biochar becomes a key player in safeguarding the delicate balance of our natural world.

Fostering Biodiversity and Environmental Conservation

The implications of biochar in fostering biodiversity extend beyond individual ecosystems, making it a crucial component of broader environmental conservation efforts. By nurturing diverse habitats and supporting resilient ecosystems, biochar contributes to the preservation of critical biodiversity hotspots. Additionally, the positive impact of biochar on biodiversity aligns with the fundamental goal of environmental conservation, highlighting its potential in mitigating the loss of species and habitats. Through its role in fostering biodiversity, biochar becomes a powerful tool in the global fight to protect and conserve our natural heritage.

In understanding the profound connection between biochar, healthier ecosystems, and environmental conservation, we uncover the potential for biochar to be a driving force in supporting the preservation and restoration of biodiversity. This chapter offers a comprehensive exploration of how biochar's impact on biodiversity underpins its broader role in environmental sustainability, leveraging its potential to create a greener and more biodiverse future.

The link between biochar and biodiversity also extends to the conservation of natural habitats. As healthy soils support a diverse range of plant species, they can create a more resilient and sustainable environment for native flora and fauna. This is especially critical in areas where habitat loss and degradation have threatened the survival of numerous species. By fostering biodiversity, biochar contributes to the broader goal of environmental conservation, supporting the preservation of natural habitats and the species that depend on them for survival.

The transformative potential of biochar in supporting robust ecosystems is evident in diverse habitats across Kenya. From the rich, biodiverse lands surrounding Nairobi to the coastal ecosystems near Mombasa, the impact of biochar on biodiversity is palpable. These thriving ecosystems stand as testaments to the positive influence of biochar on the environment, offering hope and inspiration for the conservation of biodiversity on a global scale.

Biochar, with its unparalleled ability to enhance soil health and fertility, plays a critical role in maintaining healthy, diverse habitats and promoting the resilience of natural ecosystems. As biochar enriches the soil, it fosters an environment conducive to the proliferation of diverse plant and microbial life. This flourishing biodiversity, in turn, supports the intricate web of life within the ecosystem, ensuring its stability and vitality. This interconnectedness highlights the crucial role of biochar in nurturing nature's diversity and underscores its potential as a powerful tool in environmental conservation efforts.

In rural communities outside Kenyan cities like Nairobi and Mombasa, biochar has demonstrated its ability to transform degraded soils into thriving ecosystems. Once infertile lands have been revitalized through the application of biochar, leading to the resurgence of diverse plant species and the return of a rich, vibrant habitat. This transformation has not only benefited the environment but has also had a tangible impact on the communities living in these areas. As the ecosystem regains its health, local communities have witnessed an increase in the availability of food sources, renewable resources, and economic opportunities. The ethical and practical aspect of local wealth creation is an essential part of the biochar revolution, as it ensures that the benefits of biodiversity support are felt at a grassroots level.

Furthermore, the significance of biodiversity support is amplified in the context of the global economy, where carbon credits are playing an increasingly substantial role. The positive environmental impact of biochar in nurturing biodiversity contributes to the accumulation of carbon credits, further highlighting its value in the global marketplace. As the world acknowledges the urgency of addressing climate change, initiatives that promote biodiversity and healthy ecosystems are increasingly valuable. By nurturing biodiversity and supporting the resilience of natural ecosystems, biochar is solidifying its place in the international carbon credit economy, adding both ecological and economic value to its already impressive repertoire.

The unique ability of biochar to promote biodiversity is a testament to its capacity to bring about lasting, positive change in the natural world. This transformation is not only crucial for the health of ecosystems but also holds the potential to uplift communities and contribute to the global effort towards combating climate change. The local success stories in Kenya continue to underscore the profound impact of biochar in nurturing biodiversity and supporting ecosystems, inspiring a wave of optimism and fervour in the fight for environmental conservation. As we delve deeper into the impact of biochar on biodiversity, the imperative for its widespread adoption becomes increasingly evident, presenting an opportunity not only for ecological betterment but also for ethical and profitable participation in global efforts towards sustainability.

Fostering Biodiversity through Biochar

The impact of biochar on biodiversity is nothing short of remarkable. By creating a nurturing environment for diverse flora and fauna, biochar plays a fundamental role in supporting the resilience and strength of natural ecosystems. It fosters biodiversity by providing a foundation for healthy, balanced habitats, contributing to environmental conservation on a larger scale. Understanding how biochar fosters biodiversity offers us a closer look at the interconnectedness of ecological systems and the vital role of sustainable practices in preserving our planet.

The Biodiversity Model: A Closer Look

The biodiversity model for biochar is a comprehensive framework that acknowledges the myriad ways in which biochar supports and enhances natural ecosystems. At its core, the model outlines how biochar augments soil fertility, thereby promoting the growth of a wide array of plant species. This, in turn, supports diverse insect and animal life, creating a thriving ecosystem. The model delves into the specific ways in which the introduction of biochar to soil alters its characteristics, making it more conducive to a rich and diverse population of organisms.

Dynamics and Implications

In essence, the biodiversity model for biochar operates as a living, breathing soil-ecosystem in its own right. It embodies the interconnectedness of natural systems and emphasizes the invaluable impact of preserving and nurturing diverse life forms. With a focus on maintaining equilibrium and supporting a wide range of flora and fauna, the model underlines the delicate balance of natural habitats and the potential for biochar to restore and uphold this balance.

Practically speaking, this model directly relates to the environmental conservation goals outlined in the overarching narrative of our discussion. By fostering biodiversity, biochar contributes to the preservation of natural ecosystems, ensuring that they thrive and remain resilient in the face of global challenges. This has both local and global implications, as the thriving ecosystems contribute to global carbon sequestration efforts, earning carbon credits that bolster the local economy while uplifting communities.

Promotion of Local Wealth Creation

By uncapping the potential of biochar to foster biodiversity, we not only support the intrinsic value of diverse ecosystems but also unleash the economic opportunities that stem from such initiatives. As thriving ecosystems contribute to carbon sequestration efforts, the potential for generating carbon credits becomes a viable avenue for local wealth creation. The intersection of ecological sustainability and financial viability makes biochar an essential tool in building resilient local economies while preserving the environment.

Through this model, we illustrate the direct link between biochar, biodiversity, and the economic prosperity of the local community.

The ethical and practical implications of this approach are evident, as we not only uplift ecological systems but also empower local communities to partake in environmentally sustainable practices that contribute to the global economy.

In considering this model, one must also recognize the growing role of carbon credits in the global economy, especially within the context of the ongoing climate crisis, and the potential of financial markets to supercharge the rate of biochar burial. By fostering biodiversity and supporting carbon sequestration efforts, biochar stands as a beacon of hope and practicality, shaping a future where environmental conservation and economic prosperity go hand in hand.

In nurturing nature's diversity, we witness the profound impact of healthier soils and the role of **biochar** in fostering robust ecosystems. The connection between **healthy soils, greater biodiversity, and biochar** not only underscores its potential to support diverse habitats but also highlights its pivotal role in promoting the resilience of natural ecosystems. By nurturing biodiversity, **biochar** becomes an invaluable ally in the broader mission of environmental conservation.

As we look to the future, it's clear that fostering biodiversity through the use of **biochar** plays a crucial role in creating thriving ecosystems. By supporting the health of soils and promoting the abundance of plant and animal life, we can take thoughtful steps to strengthen the ecological tapestry within our own communities. The **positive impact of biochar** in Kenyan villages and farming communities and beyond cannot be understated, as it aligns with the growing role of **carbon credits** in the global economy while ethically and practically contributing to local wealth creation.

With a deep understanding of the powerful relationship between **healthy soils, biodiversity, and biochar**, we are better equipped to take holistic actions that positively impact the environment, enhance ecosystems, and uplift communities. As we embrace the transformative potential of **biochar**, we open new chapters in the ongoing story of environmental stewardship, laying the groundwork for a more sustainable and vibrant future for generations to come.

Chapter 7: Biochar Reduces Chemical Fertilizer Usage

A warm breeze wafted through the bustling streets of Thika, tousling the leaves of the stout trees that bravely peppered the cityscape. On a small urban farm nestled somewhere between the distant soaring buildings and the horizon, Karanja stood stoically, his gaze set upon the crumbling soil in his hands. Reflecting on the sprawling city behind him in the distance, the contrast between the firm concrete sidewalks of the town and the delicate earth under his feet was stark, each telling a story of survival in their different tongues.

The clamour of the distant city faded into a low murmur as he contemplated the wilted rows of maize before him. He remembered the whispers of old wisdom, speaking of a time when the land was hearty and giving "back in the day". Nowadays, the demand for larger yields and the relentless use of chemical fertilizers had left the soil tired, its life force sapped away. The promise of biochar, a simple solution reminiscent of the ancient terra preta he had been told about, lingered in his thoughts, rich with potential.

Karanja knew well the struggles of his fellow farmers, bound by the availability of costly imported fertilizers that fed their crops yet starved future generations of nourishment. As he turned the biochar in his hand, a granular black gold, it seemed the weight of a brighter future rested there too. This carbon-rich material, forged from the remains of agricultural waste, held a whisper of hope for healing these tired lands.

The street vendors' calls punctuated his reflections, each shoutout churning the day's hustle. It was there, amidst the scent of barbecued corn and exhaust fumes, that the idea of local wealth creation, fuelled by environmentally sound practices, took root. Karanja envisioned a community bolstered by carbon credits - an incentive for Kenyans to sustainably manage their resources, embraced and financed by the global economy, fostering both the green of crops and the jingle of golden coins as the black aerial load of carbon dioxide is removed.

His calloused hand closed gently around the biochar, a symbol of the convergence of ancient methods and modern markets, of ethics melding with practicality. And as dusk painted the distant city sky in hues of fire and tranquillity, his heart swelled with an optimistic drive. With biochar's promise, could they not only enrich the soils but also the lives of his fellow Kenyans, turning barren earth into fertile futures?

How could this transformation of agriculture reshape the prosperity of Kenya's villages and towns, harmonizing with the rhythm of the global heart that yearns for sustainability?

Reducing Chemical Fertilizer Usage: Biochar's Environmental Impact

The pivotal role of biochar in revolutionizing African agriculture through sustainable practices cannot be overstated. In Chapter 7, we delve into the transformational potential of biochar in breaking the dependency on energy-intensive chemical fertilizers. This chapter illuminates biochar's capacity to reshape agricultural landscapes, reduce environmental damage, and promote soil health. By embracing biochar, we can move towards a future where African agriculture is more harmonious with nature, thriving without the heavy ecological toll of chemical fertilizers.

Reduced Need for Chemical Fertilizers: One of the key insights of this chapter lies in biochar's capacity to reduce reliance on energy-intensive chemical fertilizers. This highlights its potential to promote more sustainable agricultural practices. By offering an effective alternative to chemical fertilizers, biochar presents an opportunity to minimize the environmental impact of farming activities and simultaneously improve soil health.

Environmental Benefits of Biochar: In the pursuit of reducing chemical fertilizer usage, biochar emerges as a champion for minimizing the ecological footprint of agricultural activities. This powerful soil amendment works in harmony with nature, enriching the earth while minimizing the disruptions caused by traditional farming techniques.

Mitigating Environmental Damage and Promoting Soil Health: By reducing the use of chemical fertilizers, biochar contributes substantially to mitigating environmental damage caused by agricultural activities. The chapter underscores how biochar fosters enriched, healthier soil - a critical foundation for sustainable agriculture.

In addition to these crucial insights, "Chapter 7" offers a carefully detailed step-by-step process for conducting biochar field trials, providing invaluable guidance for researchers, agricultural extension agents, and farmers interested in studying the impact of biochar on their crops and soils.

Step-by-Step Process for Conducting Biochar Field Trials

The chapter encompasses a meticulous approach to utilizing biochar as a soil amendment, promoting sustainable agricultural practices across African landscapes. The process unfolds as follows:

1. **Select Study Sites:** Choose diverse study sites representing different soil types, cropping systems, and climate conditions, procuring permission from local authorities or landowners.

2. **Design Experimental Plots:** Divide each study site into multiple, equally sized plots, randomizing the allocation of treatments to minimize bias.

3. **Prepare Experimental Treatments:** Determine biochar application rates and apply treatments with precision and uniformity to assess the dose-response relationship.

4. **Implement Control Treatments:** Allocate control plots for comparison and implement other control treatments based on research objectives.

5. **Monitor and Collect Data:** Set up rigorous monitoring systems to assess various parameters throughout the growing season and collect data from each plot with consistency.

6. **Analyse and Interpret Results:** Utilize statistical software to analyse collected data, interpret results based on statistical significance, and consider long-term sustainability.

7. **Communicate and Disseminate Findings:** Prepare comprehensive reports or research papers summarizing trial results, present findings at relevant platforms, and publish results to contribute to existing knowledge. *(we are indebted to Sweden's Lund University for their biochar trials in Kenya and results, which frankly exceeded my expectations).

This comprehensive process equips agricultural stakeholders with the tools necessary to evaluate the impact of biochar on their crops and soils. By following these steps, researchers, extension agents, and farmers can contribute to the understanding and adoption of biochar for sustainable agricultural practices, unravelling its potential to bring about an environmental and agricultural revolution in Africa.

The roadmap outlined in this chapter fortifies the monumental potential of biochar in transforming African agriculture, fostering approaches that nurture the earth and ensure sustainable food production.

This chapter underscores the critical role biochar can play in reducing chemical fertilizer usage, promoting sustainability, and revitalizing agricultural practices across the African continent. By embracing biochar, we can cultivate a more harmonious relationship with the earth and pave the way for a greener, more prosperous future.

By grasping biochar's capacity to reduce reliance on energy-intensive chemical fertilizers and promote sustainable agricultural practices, we uncover a crucial solution to the environmental challenges faced by agricultural communities. This game-changing insight underscores the pivotal role biochar plays in transforming agricultural practices towards a more sustainable and ecologically friendly direction. The reduction of chemical fertilizer usage not only lessens the environmental impact of farming but also nurtures healthier, more resilient soils in the long run.

Biochar's ability to reduce the need for chemical fertilizers has far-reaching implications, particularly in the context of Kenya's agricultural landscape. As we delve into this pivotal aspect, we unlock the potential for local farming communities around Nairobi, Kisumu, and Mombasa, to thrive sustainably while simultaneously mitigating environmental degradation. The ramifications of this shift extend beyond local landscapes, influencing the global economy as the demand for sustainable agricultural products continues to rise. Here, in the agricultural heartlands of Kenya, the ripple effect of incorporating biochar into farming practices can be felt on an international scale through the growing role of carbon credits in the global economy.

Reducing the reliance on chemical fertilizers is not only about sustainable agricultural practices but also about ethical and practical local wealth creation. By adopting biochar as a viable alternative, agricultural communities in Nakuru, Eldoret, and Thika become active contributors to a greener, more sustainable future. This shift empowers individuals and communities to take control of their environmental impact, making a tangible difference within their own surroundings. In doing so, the ethical imperative of preserving the ecological balance for future generations becomes intertwined with a practical pursuit of building local wealth and self-sufficiency.

Fire To Life

The shift in focus from a reliance on chemical fertilizers to sustainable agricultural practices is not merely a trend; it is a necessity. It is a call to action, resonating with smallholder farmers around Kitale, Malindi, and Lamu who are eager to embrace practices that enable environmental preservation and economic sustainability. This transformative path presents a compelling narrative of hope and progress for these communities, as they become champions of a more sustainable future for themselves and the world at large.

Continue reading as we explore how the environmental benefits of biochar extend far beyond agricultural activities, offering insights into minimizing the ecological footprint and promoting soil health.

Biochar's impact on the environment is integral to understanding its potential for revolutionizing agricultural practices in Kenya and beyond. By minimizing the ecological footprint of agricultural activities, biochar offers a pathway to sustainable farming that benefits the environment and local communities. Through fervent commitment to enhancing ecosystems, biochar advocates are championing a cause that has the potential to uplift communities and create positive change, in terms of employment creation/economic earnings as well as food security and reducing Carbon Dioxide levels in the atmosphere.

In Kenya, the use of biochar has the potential to not only reduce the dependency on chemical fertilizers but also to mitigate environmental damage caused by their overuse. This reduction in chemical fertilizer usage can lead to a significant decrease in greenhouse gas emissions, thereby contributing to a healthier and more sustainable environment. Through the implementation of biochar, farmers can play an active role in reducing the ecological footprint of their agricultural activities, fostering a balanced coexistence with the environment.

The global economy is increasingly recognizing the value of carbon credits, with a growing emphasis on the importance of sustainable and environmentally friendly practices. By integrating biochar into agricultural systems, Kenyan farmers have the opportunity to participate in the carbon credit market, generating additional income while contributing to a more sustainable planet. This shift towards ethical and practical wealth creation ties directly into the broader movement towards environmental sustainability—creating a ripple effect that resonates far beyond local communities, reaching all the way to Hong Kong and Los Angeles.

When it comes to minimizing the ecological footprint of mankind, the application of biochar provides actionable steps that lead to a significant reduction in environmental impact for anyone interested in doing so. The long-term benefits of this sustainable agricultural practice ripple out into the global ecosystem, making a profound impact on the fight against climate change and environmental degradation. As we explore the environmental benefits of biochar, it's crucial to understand the far-reaching impact of sustainable farming practices, offering a potential solution to the urgent environmental challenges we face.

In the Kenyan context, biochar's role in minimizing the ecological footprint of agricultural activities presents a compelling narrative of success and progress. As we embrace inclusivity in discussing environmental benefits, it becomes evident that biochar has the potential to uplift communities and empower individuals to make a positive change. By highlighting success stories and victories tied to the implementation of biochar, we can bolster the impact of sustainable farming practices, further inspiring and motivating readers to take part in this revolutionary approach.

The aromatic scent of freshly tilled soil in Kenyan fields becomes a poignant symbol of the transformation brought about by sustainable farming practices. Through grounding readers in the tangible results of biochar implementation, this form of storytelling aims to embody the positive outcomes and potential that biochar presents. By weaving these narratives into the discussion of environmental benefits, we create a relatable and impactful dialogue that resonates universally.

Biochar's role in promoting soil health and mitigating environmental damage is a crucial aspect of sustainable agriculture. By integrating biochar into agricultural practices, farmers can not only achieve higher crop yields but also contribute to the rehabilitation of degraded soils. This solution-oriented approach not only benefits the immediate ecosystem but also has far-reaching positive effects on the global environment. The integration of biochar can offer actionable steps that lead to long-term soil health and environmental restoration.

In Kenya, for example, the use of biochar has shown promising results in promoting soil health. Farmers in peri-urban and rural areas alike have embraced the practice, recognizing biochar's potential to restore soil fertility and reduce the need for chemical fertilizers. This shift in agricultural practices aligns with the global movement towards sustainable farming methods, emphasizing the ethical and practical aspect of local wealth creation. By reducing reliance on chemical fertilizers, biochar assists in minimizing the ecological footprint of agricultural activities while simultaneously uplifting communities economically.

The integration of biochar into agricultural practices fosters inclusivity, providing a sustainable solution that spans different countries, cultures and contexts. From the bustling farming towns to the remote rural farming communities, to the busy city of New York, the benefits of biochar contribute universally to soil health, environmental restoration and atmospheric reduction of CO_2 and methane. This universal inclusivity not only widens the reach of the message but also showcases the adaptability of biochar in diverse agricultural settings. The simplicity of the language used in promoting biochar fosters accessibility, ensuring that the benefits are clear to all farmers, regardless of their level of experience.

In conclusion, the integration of biochar into agricultural practices holds the key to promoting soil health, mitigating environmental damage, atmospheric CO_2 removal and contributing to the global effort towards environmental preservation of biodiversity. Its adoption offers profound insights for farmers seeking sustainable solutions, with the potential to create a positive impact on both local ecosystems and the global environment.

As we conclude this chapter, it's clear that **biochar has the potential to revolutionize agricultural practices** by reducing the heavy dependence on energy-intensive chemical fertilizers. This shift not only promotes more sustainable and environmentally friendly farming methods but also contributes significantly to mitigating environmental damage and promoting soil health. The power of biochar lies in its ability to minimize the ecological footprint of agricultural activities, opening up a world of possibilities for a healthier, more vibrant planet with greater biodiversity.

In Kenyan farming towns and rural communities, farmers are beginning to realize the incredible impact of biochar on their agricultural practices. By embracing biochar, they not only enhance their crop yield and soil health but also make a remarkable contribution to the environment. **The potential for local wealth creation through biochar usage is immense, as it aligns with the growing role of carbon credits in the global economy.** This ethically sound practice not only benefits local communities but also aligns with global initiatives to combat climate change.

As we move forward, it's crucial to recognize the positive trajectory biochar offers for the future. Embracing biochar and reducing reliance on chemical fertilizers is not just an environmental necessity, it's a pathway towards more sustainable and prosperous communities. By harnessing the power of biochar, we can create a world where agricultural practices go hand in hand with environmental preservation, leading to a brighter future for all.

Chapter 8: Biochar as a Renewable Energy Source

(We differentiate charcoal made from Agric wastes and woody weeds using modern kilns from that very destructive type made by chopping indigenous forests using TEK – Traditional Earth Kilns – yields are 30% for modern kilns compared to 7% for the TEK).

The evening sun, a lustrous arc-shaped ember perched on the horizon, cast its farewell glow across Mombasa, Kenya. Abdi stood in the middle of his family's modest farm, the earth under his feet rich with the promise of renewal, his hands coarse and callused from years of coaxing life from the stubborn soil. In the distance, trucks trundled across the highway, their engines grumbling a dirge for the dying light.

The acrid smell of burnt plastic waste from neighbouring lands stung Abdi's nostrils, an unpleasant reminder of energy solutions yet tethered to old, polluting ways. His gaze shifted to the bag of charcoal by his feet—black, dusty, the remnants of a new method pyrolysis trial that promised greater yields. The conversion of agricultural waste to biochar using a new kiln providing renewable fuel, a project that seemed just as much alchemy as science to the local farmers, was Abdi's newly found crusade.

The journey had begun not as a quest for innovation but as a necessity. With fossil fuel prices skyrocketing, a depreciating Kenya shilling meaning anything imported has increased in price commensurately, and access to cooking gas and kerosene inconsistent at best vanishing for weeks at worst, the community's need for sustainable energy had become acute. The mangroves they used to harvest were long gone, beach erosion was common, the fish breeding grounds and nurseries had also gone, and that most lucrative of incomes, prawn fishing – harvests from the sea had dwindled. In Abdi's mind, biochar held the key to unlocking an energy source that lay dormant in their very own backyards, turning organic waste into wealth, nurturing the soil it came from, and breathing life into the lands hollowed by chemical fertilizers. He remembered how his late father would lament the declining soil health, lower fishing yields, an inheritance squandered. But where there was biochar, there might be hope, since by relieving pressure on the Mangrove forests, they could be replanted and recover, hopefully the trees would act as fish nurseries once again. It had been over a decade since he had last caught and eaten mangrove snails, once easily gathered at low tide.

This evening was different; a trial burn was underway. Flames whispered through the retort kiln, an efficient oven designed to smoulder rather than blaze. Abdi knew that the pyrolysis process not only produced biochar but also released a syngas—a reflective gift of energy that could be harnessed. His heart drummed with the rhythm of opportunity, each beat an echo of possibility against the challenges carved into his daily existence.

Fire To Life

The crisp bite of the night air began to creep in, and with it, children's laughter as they raced through the fields, ignorant of the gravity that their future was being gambled upon. The warm light from the flickering flames danced in their eyes, pulling Abdi away from his thoughts, drawing him back to the present.

The community gathered, the fire from the experimental pyrolysis unit painting hope on their faces in shades of orange and gold. They spoke of change, of reducing reliance on the low grade charcoal and firewood from cutting mangrove forests that blackened lungs and futures alike, of local wealth creation and keeping their sons and daughters close, anchored to the land by prosperity rather than necessity. The traditional methods of making charcoal yielded 7% using big chunks of wood, the smaller twigs, stalks all burned away to nothing. Now, using this new technology made from locally available used oil drums, the smaller twigs were being changed into charcoal at 33% yield. What was once being left to rot away was now a valuable fuel source.

Abdi's heart swelled. Tonight, the farm wasn't just growing crops; it was cultivating energy autonomy from waste. As the trial burn waned and the first batch of biochar was quenched, the potential for carbon credits—financial rewards for sequestering carbon dioxide—seemed a tangible dream, a bridge between ethical resource management and the global economy. He had planted mangroves before, but the community project was abandoned when they realised that for every 3 seedlings they planted, they were harvesting 10 mature trees for firewood and charcoal.

Standing amidst his community, Abdi felt the fusion of old world and new—a confluence of ancient soil and contemporary science. He envisioned future gatherings fuelled by biochar, its energy illuminating homes, empowering communities, and maybe, just maybe, lighting the spark for similar revelations worldwide. He spoke very firmly about using this new type of charcoal instead, then to mark the boundaries of the old mangrove swamps and forests and replant and protect them so the fish and prawns would return.

But as the night drew its curtain around them, leaving only the stars to speculate on their success or failure, a thought lingered in the minds of all present: Could this humble blend of earth, sea and fire truly forge a path to a sustainable future? He walked home with a smile…

Igniting Change: Biochar as a Renewable Energy Source

In the pursuit of a sustainable future, the significance of improving yields from existing renewable energy sources using new methods cannot be overstated. Across the globe, communities are searching for ways to transition from fossil fuels to cleaner, renewable energy options. In Africa, many are reverting back to charcoal as cooking gas and kerosene become increasingly expensive. It is within this context that the role of biochar as a renewable energy source becomes profoundly vital. In this pivotal chapter, we delve into the multifaceted benefits of biochar in the context of renewable energy, with a specific focus on the potential to reduce reliance on fossil fuels, particularly in local communities too poor to afford cooking gas, or too remote for kerosene to be a viable fuel.

The chapter shoulders the responsibility of unravelling the potential of biochar as a renewable energy source, highlighting its alignment with sustainable development goals. Biochar, derived from the improved pyrolysis process, stands as a beacon of hope for communities seeking alternative energy solutions that not only reduce their environmental impact but also trigger positive economic and social dynamics. It's here, in the power of biochar to ignite change, that the true green potential of Africa comes to light. Charcoal made from trees: 50 years to grow. 7% yield in a TEK. Biochar made using improved kilns like TLUD, BLDD or just the Kon-Tiki Flame Front kiln, yields between 25% to 33%.

To put this into perspective: Kenyans cut 20 million indigenous trees per year to make charcoal. Simply by changing from the TEK to a TLUD or BLDD, the yield moves from 7% to 30%, meaning trees harvested reduce from 20million to 5 million, a saving of 15 million trees per year. This is based on Kenya's charcoal production figure of 2Mn to 4Mn tonnes, we are using the lower figure. By replacing traditional charcoal with renewable charcoal, we will save 20Mn+ trees per year.

Fire To Life

The journey through this chapter is an exploration of the tangible ways in which modern biochar can alleviate the burden of fossil fuel dependence and address deforestation. It addresses the pressing need for cleaner and more sustainable energy systems and offers a deeper understanding of how biochar can serve as a catalyst for this transition. As we journey through the potential of biochar in reducing reliance on fossil fuels, particularly in local communities, a new vista of sustainability opens up—encompassing not only environmental stewardship but also local wealth creation and regional stability.

Weaving together the intricate threads of biochar's potential as a renewable energy source, this chapter showcases a vision of holistic and inclusive development. It encourages readers to recognize the power of biochar in not just mitigating environmental impact, but also in uplifting communities and fostering a sense of shared prosperity. By providing a well-researched and profound insight, this chapter sparks a fire of hope, not just for the environment, but for the people and the economies that stand to benefit from the renewable energy potential of biochar.

The responsibility to cultivate a sustainable future falls on the shoulders of each individual and each community, even deep with a densely populated city. As this chapter unfolds, it propels readers into action, offering a clear path towards embracing biochar as a renewable energy source. It calls for a fervent commitment to enhancing ecosystems, uplifting communities, and advocating for cleaner, more sustainable energy systems. Through expertly crafted insights and data-rich analysis, the chapter champions the cause of embracing biochar not merely as a renewable energy source, but as a transformative force for positive change.

The narratives woven within this chapter expertly balance immediacy with future benefits, showcasing the potential for biochar to not only address current challenges but to build a foundation for thriving, resilient communities. It isn't just a matter of recognizing the potential of biochar in reducing reliance on fossil fuels and reducing deforestation; it's about embracing biochar as a sustainable energy solution that nurtures a brighter, greener future for all.

By laying out problems succinctly and offering actionable steps that lead to resolution, this chapter serves as a guide for readers to play an active role in unlocking Africa's green potential. The insights drawn from diverse cultures and contexts widen the reach of the message, fostering a deep sense of compassion and understanding for various experiences. As the chapter unfolds, it embraces a charismatic conversational style, inspiring readers to recognize their role in making a positive change and authentically nurturing their authority through profound insights.

The implications of this discussion extend far beyond theoretical realms, extending into tangible, actionable strategies for leveraging biochar as a renewable energy source. It offers a roadmap towards embracing inclusive and sustainable energy systems, bringing readers closer to the very heart of *Fire To Life: Africa's Biochar Potential Unleashed*. Through this insightful and motivational lens, the chapter paints a vivid picture of positive outcomes and the potential for transformative change, demonstrating the power of biochar in shaping a green, sustainable, and prosperous future for Africa and the world at large.

Set against the backdrop of Kenya's ever-evolving energy landscape, biochar emerges as a beacon of hope, offering a multifaceted solution to pressing sustainable development goals. As we explore the potential of biochar as a renewable energy source, a world of possibilities unfolds, each one intricately intertwined with the betterment of our environment, communities, and economies. The energy potential 'generated' from biochar production via pyrolysis presents an opportunity to drastically reduce reliance on fossil fuels and indigenous forest charcoal. This seismic shift not only lessens our carbon footprint but also paves the way for local wealth creation and a sustainable, thriving future.

The Intersection of Sustainability and Energy

A complex problem requires complex solutions – renewable biochar is a good foundation/pillar towards achieving lower CO_2 levels in the air. Achieving sustainability calls for innovative solutions that can address multiple environmental and societal challenges simultaneously. The dividends paid by utilizing biochar as a renewable energy source extend far beyond mere energy production. Biochar, with its carbon sequestration capabilities, offers a path towards mitigating climate change, enriching soil quality, and fostering sustainable agriculture. Furthermore, the potential of biochar in reducing deforestation, a common practice for fuel in many local communities is to go to the nearby forest and cut trees for firewood and charcoal, renewable biochar aligns with overarching efforts to preserve our natural ecosystems.

Empowering Local Communities

The importance of reducing reliance on fossil fuels is magnified in local communities, especially in Kenya, and I dare say Africa. The EU has led the way in renewable energy, using "mega projects like windfarms and giant solar farms". Buying fuel is usually the single-biggest Forex expense and even distorts Forex rates, as countries buy US$ to import energy. With biochar's promise of clean, renewable energy, we can lift communities out of energy poverty, offering them access to alternative, sustainable energy solutions. By engaging local communities in the production and utilization of biochar, we create opportunities for economic empowerment, foster entrepreneurship, and provide the means for a brighter future. We are not going to discuss biochar fuelled steam generators for electricity generation here, this is a distinct possibility for rural electricity generation.

The Promise of Carbon Credits

The global economy is increasingly recognizing the value of sustainability, with carbon credits playing an instrumental role in incentivizing environmentally friendly practices. As biochar production aligns with these practices, it opens doors for local communities and enterprises to access, trade, and benefit from carbon credits. This not only positions biochar as a viable vehicle for wealth creation but also underscores its ethical imperative in fostering environmental stewardship increasing biodiversity and reducing deforestation.

By recognizing the multifaceted benefits of biochar as a renewable energy source aligned with sustainable development goals, we unearth a powerful tool for positive change. This journey into the world of biochar introduces us to a sphere of influence that goes beyond energy production, channelling into the realms of environmental rejuvenation, economic upliftment, and community empowerment. As we delve deeper into the energy potential of biochar, the narrative of sustainable progress begins to unfold, illuminating the path towards a brighter, greener future for us all.

Stay with us as we further explore the potential of biochar in reducing reliance on fossil fuels, particularly in rural communities.

As communities seek to reduce reliance on fossil fuels, particularly in rural and peri-urban areas, the potential of biochar as a renewable energy source grows more evident. The impact of this sustainable energy solution in local economies cannot be understated, as it offers a pathway to self-sufficiency and environmental stewardship. Kenyan communities, outside Nairobi and Mombasa, are actively exploring the integration of biochar with the aim of promoting energy independence while reducing their carbon footprint.

The Role of Biochar in Local Energy Independence and Deforestation

In Kenya, and other African nations, the need to reduce dependence on costly and environmentally damaging fossil fuels has never been more urgent. Biochar presents an innovative solution capable of transforming organic waste into a valuable energy source. By harnessing the power of modern pyrolysis, local communities can produce biochar while simultaneously generating renewable energy, thus reducing the need for non-renewable (slow growing forest trees) resources. This dual benefit not only provides a tangible alternative to fossil fuels but also supports the economic growth of local communities through sustainable energy and forestry practices.

Incorporating Carbon Credits to Drive Sustainable Initiatives

As the global economy increasingly embraces the value of carbon credits, the integration of biochar into sustainable energy systems becomes even more attractive. Kenyan companies are strategically positioning themselves to take advantage of carbon credits, leveraging biochar production as a means to mitigate climate change and contribute to carbon sequestration efforts. The potential for earning carbon credits through biochar projects is an exciting prospect, providing an additional stream of income for local communities and reinforcing the economic viability of sustainable energy solutions.

Empowering Local Communities through Ethical Wealth Creation

The practical and ethical implications of local wealth creation through biochar production cannot be overlooked. By embracing biochar as a renewable energy source, local communities in Kenyan villages and peri-urban areas can take control of their energy needs, reducing reliance on external resources and ensuring greater resilience in the face of economic fluctuations whilst reducing deforestation. The ethical significance lies in the empowerment of these communities to become self-sufficient in energy production, thereby fostering a sense of ownership and stewardship over their environmental impact.

Strategically Positioning Biochar for Sustainable Development

The potential of biochar in reducing reliance on fossil fuels in local communities extends far beyond immediate energy needs. It aligns with broader sustainable development goals by promoting environmental responsibility, economic empowerment, and long-term ecological benefits for future generations. Kenyan rural communities, villages and other urban centres are recognizing the multifaceted value of biochar, acknowledging its potential to drive meaningful change in their energy landscapes while contributing to global efforts in combatting climate change and deforestation.

Unlocking the Potential of Biochar using Modern Pyrolysis

The process of creating biochar through modern pyrolysis is not only a means of generating renewable energy but also a demonstration of sustainable resource management. Previously agricultural and food wastes, twigs, branches were left to rot away in the fields, or in piles to compost. This creates CO_2 and methane as they decompose. By harnessing the power of such organic waste via biochar, local communities in Kenyan villages towns and cities are taking proactive steps towards environmental conservation while simultaneously providing for their energy needs. This symbiotic relationship between sustainable energy production and environmental stewardship demonstrates the transformative potential of biochar in reducing reliance on fossil fuels and advancing local economies.

The adoption of biochar as a renewable energy source is intertwined with the broader narrative of sustainability and progress. In Kenyan villages, towns and rural communities, where the effects of climate change are acutely felt, integrating biochar into energy systems is a proactive measure toward climate resilience. Through education and awareness, local communities can realize the potential of biochar in fostering sustainable development, economic prosperity, and environmental well-being.

Ultimately, by embracing biochar made from food and agricultural wastes as an alternative energy solution, local communities in Kenyan villages and towns have the opportunity to enact positive change on a global scale. The sustainable energy derived from biochar not only addresses immediate energy needs but also aligns with a vision of long-term environmental stewardship. This vision encompasses the ethical responsibility to care for the planet and the practical necessity of creating viable, sustainable economies. As biochar emerges as a pivotal player in the renewable energy landscape, its potential to transform the trajectory of local communities is boundless.

Fire To Life

Biochar holds immense potential as a renewable energy source, igniting change in local communities and protecting forests across Kenya and beyond. Through the process of modern pyrolysis, it offers a sustainable solution that reduces reliance on fossil fuels and forest products, benefiting both the environment and the economy. The multifaceted benefits of biochar align perfectly with the sustainable development goals, showcasing its capacity to effect positive change on a global scale. By recognizing the potential of biochar in providing alternative energy solutions, we pave the way for cleaner, more sustainable energy systems that uplift communities while safeguarding the planet's forests for future generations.

As we look to the future, it's crucial to embrace the role of biochar in reducing carbon emissions when buried, reducing deforestation when used as a fuel and its growing significance in the global economy. The emerging carbon credit market presents an opportunity for local communities in Kenyan villages and rural communities to not only contribute to mitigating climate change and protect forests but also to generate revenue through sustainable practices. By producing biochar, these communities not only reduce their carbon footprint but also create a valuable commodity in the form of carbon credits which can be sold worldwide, bolstering their local economies and contributing to the global effort to combat climate change.

Furthermore, the practical aspect of local wealth creation through biochar production cannot be overlooked. By harnessing the energy potential of biochar, communities can reduce their dependency on expensive fossil fuels, eliminate the use of damaging forest-sourced fuels and instead invest in a renewable, cost-effective energy source. This not only leads to significant cost savings but also empowers communities to take control of their energy needs, fostering self-reliance and sustainability.

In the grand scheme of things, understanding the potential of biochar as a renewable energy source is not just about embracing a new technology; it's about embracing a new way of living. It's about recognizing our interconnectedness with the environment and the pivotal role we play in cultivating a more sustainable future. By harnessing the power of biochar, we kindle a brighter path towards cleaner energy, healthier ecosystems, preserved forests and thriving communities across Kenya and the world.

Chapter 9: Economic Opportunities from Biochar

The sun had just finished tracing its golden path across the Kenyan sky when Okello, had hit that sweet spot in the day where the heat seemed to simmer down to a friendly warmth. His eyes, reflecting a sheen from the sun's parting kiss, looked out over the expanse of his modest farm on the outskirts of Nakuru. There, piles of agricultural waste were testament to his recent harvest: a bounty and a burden all at once. The detritus of maize stalks whispered secrets of untapped wealth, secrets Okello was keen to uncover.

In the quiet hum of the late afternoon, he turned over in his mind the potential of these organic remnants. They spoke of a transformative power; not just for his land, but for his entire community. Okello had heard of biochar, a substance wrought from the pyrogenic conversion of this biomass, a process both simple and profound, turning what was once waste into wealth. The farm's scent of earth mixed with a tinge of residual smoke from wood-fuelled cooking fires in the distance—a smell that was evocative of cycles old and new, but he suspected deep down, has caused his grandmother's blindness and how own mother had eye problems.

He recalled the meeting last week, where a group of agricultural experts introduced biochar to the local farmers. They explained how its use could not only improve soil fertility but also sequester carbon, a detail that caught everyone's attention. They spoke of carbon credits and a global economy that was increasingly putting a value on such activities; Kenyan farmers could be part of this valuable burgeoning market.

Such endeavour required investment, yes, but also a collective effort that could steer the community towards a future that was at once more prosperous and sustainable. The experts shared testimonies of other rural areas where biochar had revitalized failing soils, reinvigorated local economies, and made farmers key players in the battle against climate change.

As Okello turned the brittle stalks over in his hands, his thoughts danced between doubt and hope. Whilst the potential was clearly there, could they truly harness it? The promise of biochar offered more than just an opportunity; it presented a challenge to which he felt both excited and unprepared. To convince his community to adopt a new practice, transform their waste, and embrace this chance—was a task of great weight. But the potential revenue from the production and application of biochar, and the lure of carbon credits, could indeed tip the balance.

Normally he would leave the maize stalks to rot in a corner and decompose, or lay them in between the rows of maize and they would disappear over the course of a few months, he was never sure what happened. Now he had been told, they were decomposing into

Fire To Life

CO_2 and methane. By actively making biochar, he could lock their goodness into his soil permanently and make his soil more fertile.

The chirps of evening crickets blended with the distant laughter of children, pulling Okello back from his contemplations. The vibrant community life around him, the very fabric of rural Kenyan society, he thought, was ripe for such empowerment. With biochar, they could tread a path of self-determination, building a more resilient economic future grounded in their agricultural heritage.

He imagines a generation of young Kenyans, once drawn to the siren call of city life, now finding reasons to stay, to invest their labour in the land of their forebears. And what more, he muses, the financial gains could enable the construction of schools, clinics, and other community benefits.

As the stars began to punctuate the twilight, Okello realized that each compound light from above mirrored a spark of possibility on the ground. This could be the inception of their own stars—stories of success born from the soil and agriculture from within his community.

As the hues of dusk settled over his farm, a thought lingered in the coolness of the evening: could the key to both sustaining his way of life and the planet lie in this ebony granule, known as biochar, cradled in the farmer's rugged palm? How heavily could the scales tip towards prosperity, should they grasp the economic and ecological lifeline this charcoal doppelgänger offered?

Harnessing Rural Prosperity: Unleashing Economic Potential through Biochar

Unlocking Africa's Green Potential is an ambitious endeavour that hinges on harnessing the economic opportunities embedded in sustainable practices. In Chapter 9, we delve deep into the economic significance of biochar production and application, particularly in rural regions where agricultural waste is abundant. This critical exploration reveals the potential for biochar not only to mitigate environmental degradation but also to catalyse local economic development, creating jobs and viable revenue streams. This insight underscores the broader socio-economic impact of biochar, highlighting its potential to uplift the poorest communities and foster sustainable livelihoods.

The convergence of environmental conservation and wealth creation emerges as a central theme within this exploration, reinforcing the idea that profitability leads to sustainable practices can serve as catalysts for long term economic growth. As we unravel the profound potential of biochar in generating job opportunities and fostering revenue streams, the significance of community empowerment and rural prosperity comes to the fore. This chapter is an invaluable compass for those seeking to navigate the terrain of biochar production with a vision for both environmental, economic and human impact.

Unveiling Economic Opportunities:

As we journey through this chapter, you will uncover how the production and application of biochar hold the key to creating economic opportunities, especially in rural settings. The abundant availability of agricultural waste and waste biomass (on a gigatonne level) presents a promising resource for biochar production, paving the way for economic empowerment and local wealth creation. This discovery marks a pivotal moment in recognizing the intrinsic economic potential embedded within sustainable practices.

Fostering Local Economic Development:

The potential of biochar in generating jobs and harvesting viable international revenue streams for local economic development is unveiled with vibrant clarity. The symbiotic relationship between environmental sustainability and economic growth is exemplified in the opportunities that biochar presents, laying the groundwork for a holistic approach to ecosystem preservation and community prosperity. The ultimate beneficiary, is of course humanity via reduced CO_2 levels in the atmosphere.

Empowerment and Prosperity:

Furthermore, we delve into the ways in which biochar supports community empowerment and contributes to rural prosperity, underscoring the transformative power of sustainable practices in uplifting livelihoods. By reflecting on tangible examples of how biochar interventions have catalysed local economic growth, we illuminate the path toward a future where environmental stewardship is intrinsically linked with local wealth creation and prosperity.

This chapter offers more than just theoretical understanding; it provides a roadmap for action, (what I have done, is not the only way, maybe not the best way, but a way) offering a step-by-step process for establishing a biochar production facility at a larger scale. This comprehensive guide is designed for entrepreneurs, organizations, or government agencies interested in commercial biochar production.

The Art of Building Prosperity: A Step-by-Step Guide

This transformative process is a testament to the practicality and immediate applicability of biochar production in nurturing economic opportunities and environmental sustainability. Embark on this journey of establishment with resolute determination, armed with a clear objective to harness the economic potential of biochar. This is what I have noted – maybe not the best, maybe not definitive, but a good enough foundation for anyone starting along the journey. Start small, but start. Once you are "on the ground, in the field" – there will be no end of large scale commercial farmer interested in you improving their soil fertility and structure.

1 Crafted for Action:

With a clear purpose at its core, this step-by-step process presents a pragmatic guide to establishing a biochar production facility at a larger scale. Each sequential step paves the way for tangible progress, holding firm to the overarching objective of catalysing rural prosperity through biochar. The good news is – the tools are rudimentary, and can be hired-borrowed-fabricated at a small scale if necessary. At its most basic, $10 of tooling, dig a conical shaped hole in the ground = a basic biochar factory. The rest, is "spokes and gold-plated alloy rims on a wheel already invented 10,000+ years ago".

2 Actionable and Adaptive:

The process unfolds with actionable clarity, ensuring that each step is both feasible and adaptable to varying landscapes and contexts. Each stage is imbued with the potential for immediate impact, affirming the immediate and transformative power infused within sustainable economic ventures. Biochar can be made using a hole in the ground, (flame front or flame curtain – AKA Kon-Tiki) and a shovel. At its very basic it is a $10 operating cost. In Kenya we make 2million tonnes using machetes, shovels leaves and earth – maybe $20 per kiln-firing operation.

3 Guided by Evaluation and Feedback:

A mechanism for evaluating the results and providing feedback underscores the dynamic nature of this process. It is a living, breathing framework that invites introspection, adaptation, and continuous improvement, ensuring that the path to prosperity is firmly rooted in self-assessment and evolution. As you start, the biochar may be "low quality (low temperatures), it may be ashy (too much oxygen) there is no substitute for experience. With all my education I would be beaten hands-down by any illiterate experienced charcoal maker in the bush. The best judge of the quality of your biochar – is a charcoal dealer when you ask him or her to buy it. They will list everything wrong. Do not be offended, go back and fix it, for you are competing with people who grew up making charcoal for generations.

4 Set against a Clear Timeline:

This process is characterized by pragmatism and momentum, exemplified in a defined timeframe that ensures progress unfolds in a timely manner. Each stage is imbued with a sense of urgency, yet balanced with the assurance of meticulous preparation and execution. De-construct the processes and make sure you allocate generous timelines. They will improve and become shorter, much shorter as you gain experience. Making biochar at scale is not easy. It is dirty, it is dusty, it is bulky and frankly look at your local colliery or charcoal yard for real guidance on storage (rain) and security (theft). Location must be away from human populations, or you must have a "rain curtain or scrubber" to wash the dust out of the air (something I have never seen). But you must start, and wait for the opportunities that will inevitably arise as you grow and scale up. There will inevitably be delays, cost overruns, permits, planning, and these need to be accounted for. If you have a $100K budget for machinery, you can only order $30K in round 1, modify, adjust, tropicalize, order $20K in round 2, be incremental and deliberate or else you will be left holding $100K of non-functioning equipment. An efficient-on-paper motor might suck in charcoal dust and short itself every 3 weeks. Remember, charcoal is light and yet abrasive and conducts electricity-ish.

5 Defining Success and Resolution:

As every step unfolds, a clear vision of success guides the journey, marking the completion of the process. The culmination of each phase is not an endpoint, but a gateway to new heights of economic empowerment and environmental conservation, attaining local and global impact. This is easier than you might think, the success of any biochar operation is measured in tonnes produced, and there will be many farmers willing to trial pilots and agree to large scale offtake/dumping on their fields.

The production and application of biochar offer a plethora of economic opportunities, particularly in rural areas and farmland. As the demand for sustainable practices and renewable energy sources continues to grow, the emergence of biochar presents a promising avenue for economic prosperity. In Kenya, for example, biochar production from agricultural waste has the potential to generate revenue streams, create job opportunities, and bolster local economies. By turning organic waste into a valuable resource, biochar not only addresses environmental concerns but also contributes to the economic well-being of communities, lifting them from poverty and creating sustainable livelihoods.

Biochar production provides a unique opportunity for rural areas to capitalize on their abundant agricultural waste. By converting this waste into biochar, farmers and rural communities can generate an additional stream of income. Imagine the positive impact on a small-scale farming community in Nakuru, Kenya, where previously discarded agricultural waste is transformed into a valuable commodity, thereby creating a circular and sustainable economy. This shift not only reduces waste but also enhances the overall economic landscape, allowing for greater financial stability and resilience in rural communities.

Furthermore, the production of biochar contributes to mitigating climate change, a critical issue in today's global economy. As the world moves towards a more carbon-neutral future, the demand for carbon credits continues to rise. It will not be enough to reduce emissions, teams of players will be needed to bury CO_2 underground – whether as CO_2 or as pure Carbon (biochar). Through the production of biochar, Kenya and other African nations have the potential to partake in the growing global carbon trading market. This presents a profound opportunity for sustainable development, as rural communities can benefit from the sale of carbon credits in the global economy while simultaneously contributing to environmental preservation.

The economic potential of biochar extends beyond carbon credits, emphasizing a holistic approach to wealth creation. When implemented on a larger scale around urban centres like Nairobi or around coastal areas like Mombasa, biochar production can serve as a catalyst for job creation, enticing young innovators and entrepreneurs to explore sustainable business models based around market agriculture. Consequently, biochar holds the promise of fostering a new wave of economic innovation, further bolstering Kenya's position in the global marketplace. H.E. President Ruto has said he wants Kenya to be at the forefront of Carbon Credits, and we have the skills and expertise to do it. Whilst the political leadership is "full steam ahead", the financial markets and indeed laws and statutes, are lagging behind.

As expectations grow for a more sustainable future, the economic potential of biochar becomes even more evident. The establishment of biochar production facilities in vast, underpopulated semi-arid regions of Kenya like Turkana can provide employment for local communities, offering a path towards economic stability where opportunities were previously scarce, on a megatonne scale. This might seem counter-intuitive, but Lake Turkana is a massive under-utilized freshwater resource, and River Tana flows through the deserts of Garissa, untapped. This transformative approach to wealth creation has the potential to uplift marginalized communities, instilling a sense of hope and fostering a renewed spirit of progress.

Join us as we delve deeper into the potential of biochar in generating jobs and potential revenue streams for local economic development.

Biochar offers a plethora of economic opportunities, especially in rural areas where agricultural waste is abundant. The production and application of biochar can generate jobs, ignite local economic growth, and pave the way for potentially significant revenue streams. By harnessing the power of biochar, communities in Kenyan rural villages can cultivate sustainable livelihoods and economic prosperity while contributing to global environmental sustainability. I will reiterate – Kenya has massive underutilized water resources in the River Tana, and Lake Turkana, along with "empty land owned by pastoralists". Every heavy rains, there are floods downriver as the parched baked-solid land fails to allow the water underground. Large scale application of biochar – whether as swales or bunds or berms – will slow the water and make sure more water enters underground rather than just wash away the fertile topsoil and carry it into the Indian Ocean.

In Kenya, the production of biochar has the potential to create numerous jobs, particularly in rural areas. The process of converting agricultural waste into biochar requires semi-skilled and unskilled labour, from collecting biomass to operating biochar production equipment. This presents an opportunity to reduce unemployment rates and boost local economies. Furthermore, the demand for biochar in agricultural and environmental applications can drive further job creation, expanding employment opportunities for individuals in various sectors. It is not exclusive to men nor women, and lends itself to youth, the sector that traditionally suffers highest unemployment. Personally I classify the ability to make good charcoal/biochar a skilled artisanal profession, not any different to brewing beer, but…

The economic impact of biochar extends beyond job creation to the potential for revenue generation. Farmers and entrepreneurs can capitalize on the production and sale of biochar as a sustainable and environmentally friendly product. This creates an avenue for new businesses to emerge and thrive, leading to an increase in local economic activity. As biochar gains traction as a valuable soil amendment, its market value is expected to grow, opening up opportunities for enterprising individuals and communities to benefit financially, both from making charcoal/biochar, burying biochar and increased food production and sales.

Moreover, the utilization of biochar contributes to the empowerment of local communities and the sustainable growth of rural economies. By engaging in biochar production and application, communities in Kenyan villages can take control of their environmental impact while creating wealth in an ethical and practical manner. This aligns with the ethos of sustainable development, emphasizing the responsible management of resources to meet present needs for food and income without compromising the ability of future generations to meet their own needs.

As the global economy increasingly recognizes the importance of environmental conservation, the role of carbon credits in rewarding sustainable practices in Africa cannot be overlooked. The production and application of biochar into soil presents an opportunity for Kenyan villages to participate in the growing carbon credit market, further enhancing the economic prospects associated with biochar. The potential to earn carbon credits provides a compelling incentive for communities to embrace biochar production, serving as a tangible recognition of their contribution to global environmental sustainability.

In harnessing the economic potential of biochar, the emphasis is not solely on financial gains, but also on the promotion of ethical and sustainable wealth creation and food security within local communities. The production and application of biochar represents a profound opportunity for Kenyan villages and agricultural towns to bolster their economies while adhering to principles of responsible environmental stewardship. By embracing biochar, communities can uplift themselves economically while making meaningful contributions to the global fight against climate change and environmental degradation.

Biochar is not only a solution for environmental sustainability but also a powerful tool for community empowerment and rural prosperity in Kenyan communities, many of whom seem to be on a never-ending cycle of drought, lower production, overgrazing, bony cows and hopelessness. This usually culminates in a drift towards the bright lights of the city, and emigration to Middle-East, USA, UK and suchlike. In contrast, the economic opportunities presented by biochar locally, homegrown, are vast, and they have the potential to transform local economies and livelihoods. By understanding how biochar supports community empowerment and contributes to rural prosperity, we can unlock its full potential and create lasting change for the better.

Empowering Local Economies: One of the most significant contributions of biochar to rural prosperity is its ability to empower local economies at the very basic grass-roots level. Through the production and application of biochar, rural communities can develop revenue streams that are deeply connected to the local environment. This creates a sense of ownership and responsibility, leading to sustainable economic growth that is not dependent on external factors. I cannot stress how poor Kenyan pastoralists are, and what earning $2 to $3 per day (2023 going rates, we suggest you pay more) means to entire communities scraping by and waiting for relief food trucks.

Job Creation and Skills Development: Additionally, the production of biochar can generate employment opportunities in rural areas. From the collection of agricultural waste to the manufacturing of biochar, to fabricating welding riveting and repairing basic modern kilns, there are various stages that require skilled labour. Ironically – it takes great skill to "balance the fire" in a TEK, too little it goes out, too much you end up with ashes, but they are deemed unskilled. This presents a chance for communities to develop expertise in sustainable practices while also increasing their earning potential. This dual benefit has the power to uplift entire communities and create a sense of purpose and pride in their work.

Carbon Credits and Global Economy: With the growing role of carbon credits in the global economy, biochar presents an opportunity for communities to participate in global environmental initiatives while also reaping economic benefits. The production of biochar can lead to carbon sequestration, which has the potential to earn carbon credits. This not only incentivizes sustainable practices but also provides a direct link between local actions and global environmental efforts. Any modern conference has a raft of companies looking to buy biochar – and the world leaders in "client offtake" are the European Biochar Institute (EBI), with clients ranging from tier-1 banks to tier-1 airlines and tier-1 hotels flying their flags and banners at any EBI jamboree.

Ethical and Practical Wealth Creation: Biochar production and application offer a practical and ethical approach to wealth creation in many poor rural areas. By utilizing agricultural waste, woody weeds as a biomass resource, communities can generate income without depleting natural resources and indigenous forests. This ensures that economic growth is sustainable in the long term, preserving the environment for future generations. I will not criticise the EU-Types who clink champagne glasses and launch yet another monitoring tool, yet another AI programme yet another brokerage, and for their $50Mn will not capture 1 tonne of CO_2. The criticism is implicit – biochar is elbow-grease calloused hands sweaty dirty digging in CO_2 into the ground work.

Community Ownership and Empowerment: The process of producing and utilizing biochar fosters a sense of community ownership and empowerment, because suddenly waste biomass becomes valuable, and wasted land becomes valuable. When local resources are transformed into valuable products, it instils a sense of pride and unity in the community. This empowerment is not just economic but also social, leading to stronger, more resilient communities that are better equipped to face challenges. Land stewardship improves as a result. When people make money from the land, it is valuable, worth protecting and investing in.

Local Innovation and Entrepreneurship: The economic opportunities presented by biochar also encourage local innovation and entrepreneurship. Communities can develop unique methods for biochar production, creating a space for localized solutions and expertise. We have many examples of machinery imported from EU/China proving unsuitable, then being modified to work better. The best case is the "mesh screens" for sorting crushed charcoal – if they break, they are best replaced by heavier gauge sheet steel with holes manually drilled in using a HSS drill bit. Modern 3-phase motors are replaced with older (rewindable) single-phase motors. Extra Pulleys being welded on for rubber power transmission belts because the chain is a special size and not available locally etc. This not only stimulates economic growth but also fosters a culture of innovation and problem-solving within communities.

Sustainable Livelihoods and Environmental Stewardship: Ultimately, the economic opportunities created by biochar contribute to the establishment of sustainable livelihoods and environmental stewardship. By demonstrating the economic value of sustainable practices, biochar encourages communities to take ownership of their environment and actively participate in its preservation. A typical example is the overgrown roads in Baringo, where by turning the weeds into charcoal then biochar, what was an 18-metre wide road, now a single-track, is being reverted to 18-metre wide roads by cutting back the weeds and making biochar. One might well-ask – why was the county not maintaining the roads? As county budgets in the developed world are strained, third world counties are 10-times worse off. Biochar being commercialized means the community is paid to maintain those overgrown roads.

As we delve deeper into the potential of biochar to support community empowerment and contribute to rural prosperity, it becomes clear that this powerful solution goes beyond environmental benefits. It has the capacity to drive economic growth, foster community pride, and create lasting positive change for local economies in Kenyan villages and rural towns.

Biochar is not just about enhancing soil fertility or mitigating climate change; it is about creating **economic opportunities** that uplift communities and nurture local prosperity. As we've delved into the production and application of biochar, it's become clear that this simple yet powerful substance has the potential to transform rural areas in communities outside Nairobi, Mombasa, and Kisumu.

Fire To Life

By converting agricultural waste into a valuable resource, biochar paves the way for sustainable livelihoods and inclusive growth.

In the journey we've taken through the potential revenue streams that biochar can unlock, it's evident that this innovative approach has the capacity to generate an array of benefits, from job creation to local economic development. Whether it's through traditional farming communities or innovative urban agricultural practices, the economic benefits of biochar stand to strengthen local economies and foster resilience in the face of global challenges. I will not give definitive numbers – but in many impoverished rural communities, $2 to $3 per day is a life-saving boon.

Furthermore, as we've explored how biochar supports community empowerment, it's clear that this isn't just a concept, but a reality with tangible impacts. In Kenyan communities, biochar has the potential to shift the tides of economic disparity, offering a path toward financial independence and sustainability for marginalized communities, many of whom rely on relief food for survival.

In light of these revelations, consider the profound implications of biochar's potential for Africa and beyond. As carbon credits play an increasingly substantial role in the global economy, biochar stands as a viable avenue for not only environmental stewardship but also for the ethical and practical creation of local wealth.

As we move forward, let's harness our collective fervour and intention to drive this revolution. With the power of biochar at our fingertips, we can navigate toward a future where economic empowerment, environmental sustainability, and community prosperity converge harmoniously.

Chapter 10: Biochar Mitigates Climate Change

Amidst the industrious hum of Nairobi's burgeoning cityscape in the distance, Kioni stood surveying the expanse of his small farm—a patchwork of greenery juxtaposed against the ever-expanding concrete as people built apartments to house employees for Nairobi's offices, an hour away. It was just past noon, the sun a clear eye in the sky, unforgiving in its scrutiny. But Kioni's thoughts dwelt not on the heat but on the soil beneath his feet, teeming with life and the promise of a legacy beyond the meagre yields of past seasons.

The land, once bountiful, now yielding scant harvests, whispered secrets of change. The whispers had a name—biochar—a simple substance holding the key to reinvigorated earth. Kioni remembered the conference, where a passionate speaker had painted pictures of soil carbon storages and microorganism kingdoms with the same reverence others reserved for fine art. He thought of his children, how this could be the answer to keeping his family's land from becoming just another forgotten patch eaten by the city's hungry demand for employee housing.

In his hand, he cradled the dark, grainy biochar, a boon to his crops, to the air, to the fine balance of life. He mulled over how this charcoal, once waste, could trap carbon in a mausoleum of fertility, locking it away from the atmosphere. He had heard of carbon credits, of wealth created not through extraction, but through conservation. Could he transform his farm into a wellspring of this new "green" currency?

As he integrated the material into his soil, he thought of the methane that the ground would have expelled from rotting plant material previously, the carbon dioxide which would have leaked into the air, now ensnared as pure carbon. The practice felt not just practical but profoundly ethical—shepherding the ecological equilibrium, ensuring that his hands did not strip the land for the next generation but enhanced its fertility.

The scent of earth, rich and potent, filled the air, and Kioni watched as his workers toiled under the Kenyan sun, their labour not merely for sustenance but for healing the planet. Each granule of biochar represented a droplet of hope, a fragment of the future. As the sun traced its path towards the horizon, shadows grew long, and the farm transformed into a tableau of change. The sweat on Kioni's brow, the rhythmic movement of hands through soil, the steadfast gaze upon a field reborn—it was the embodiment of an Africa rising, one farm at a time.

His heart swelled with a cautious optimism. The path to a healthier planet was long and fraught with unseen challenges, yet the seeds of change were sown. How many other farmers across the vast Kenyan landscapes could join this green revolution? Could the choices of people like Kioni ripple outwards, bringing a tide of restoration and abundance?

In the quietening light of day, when the earth began to cool and the bustle ebbed into serenity, Kioni pondered the future. Would the world recognize the value in what he and his land offered, not just in crops, but in the currency of carbon, the wealth of a balanced earth? How soon would it be before the market for good deeds would find root in financial markets in far away places like London, Hong Kong and New York, and would it be enough to turn the tides?

Biochar's Crucial Role in Climate Change Mitigation

As we delve into Chapter 10, "Climate Warriors: Biochar's Role in Mitigating Climate Change," it becomes abundantly clear that the impact of biochar on climate change mitigation is not just a localized phenomenon. It has far-reaching implications that extend well beyond the boundaries of the regions where it is produced and used. This chapter underscores the urgency and importance of biochar's contribution to mitigating climate change by reducing greenhouse gas emissions, particularly from soil.

To reiterate, the burial of one tonne of biochar in any African village, is 3.67 tonnes of CO_2 permanently removed from the world's atmosphere. We say 3 tonnes to be conservative.

Fire To Life

The central theme of this chapter revolves around the pivotal role biochar plays in slowing down the decomposition of organic matter and preventing the release of carbon dioxide and methane into the atmosphere. This profound insight highlights the interconnectedness of soil health and climate change, illuminating the transformative potential of biochar in preserving ecological balance and planetary health.

The first key takeaway from this chapter is the **recognition of biochar's significant contribution to climate change mitigation** by reducing greenhouse gas emissions from soil, especially methane. By addressing this critical aspect, the chapter equips the reader with a deeper understanding of the pivotal role biochar plays in the fight against climate change.

The second key learning is the understanding of **how making biochar slows down, if not completely arrests the decomposition of organic matter**, thereby preventing the release of carbon dioxide and methane into the atmosphere. This insight underscores the tangible impact of biochar in arresting the escalation of greenhouse gas emissions. New scientific evidence (Hans Peter Schmidt, Hamed Sanei et. al.) suggests 25% of biochar lasts 100 years in the soil, with the remaining 75% lasting 1,000+ years. There is evidence (peer reviewed) that 76% stays for millions of years. I am happy with a 100-year delay – allowing future generations time to sort this mess out.

The chapter also provides a profound exploration of how biochar contributes to the **preservation of ecological balance** and the overarching goal of safeguarding planetary health. This comprehensive understanding of biochar's multi-faceted role serves as a clarion call to action, compelling the reader to recognize the urgency and significance of biochar in the broader context of environmental preservation.

As we navigate through this pivotal chapter, it is crucial to comprehend the overarching themes of the book, "Fire To Life: Africa's Biochar Potential Unleashed." This book seeks to provide comprehensive knowledge on biochar, particularly from Africa, and its potential impact in various areas. By the end of this transformative journey, the reader will have gained a thorough understanding of biochar and its potential for global-yet-local impact, particularly in Africa, with its untapped potential. Africa really is a sleeping giant whom we can awaken to the benefit of the whole world.

The core problem this book seeks to solve is the lack of comprehensive knowledge on biochar and its applications, which can hinder the effective harnessing of its benefits for various purposes. The emphasis on biochar's potential for carbon sequestration, soil fertility improvement, and environmental sustainability positions the reader as an active participant in leveraging biochar's transformative potential. By equipping the reader with the necessary knowledge and skills to effectively use biochar, the book empowers individuals to make a positive impact in their communities and beyond. There is no substitute for practice – in becoming an expert.

In the broader context of the global economy, the book acknowledges the growing role of carbon credits and their impact on environmental initiatives. By highlighting the ethical and practical aspect of local wealth creation through biochar, the book underscores the significance of sustainable and environmentally conscious practices in fostering economic growth. By marrying the CO2 sequestration needs of the developed world with the wasted/untapped biomass resources of Africa, we hope to make a significant difference in the climatic capture of CO_2 using trees, plants, then placing it underground safely as biochar.

Biochar's contribution to climate change mitigation by reducing greenhouse gas emissions from soil cannot be overstated. The use of biochar in agricultural practices has shown tremendous potential in sequestering carbon and reducing the release of potent greenhouse gases such as methane and nitrous oxide. This presents an incredible opportunity to address climate change by mitigating its effects, while also improving soil health and agricultural productivity.

Studies have shown that biochar can significantly reduce the emissions of methane, a major contributor to global warming, from soil by hosting methanophage bacteria. It acts as a stable carbon reservoir, effectively locking in carbon and preventing methane's release into the atmosphere via said bacteria. This aspect of biochar's role makes it an invaluable tool in the fight against climate change, offering a sustainable solution to reducing greenhouse gas emissions. There are many scientific articles, I will condense them thus: The presence of methanogens and methanotrophs is reduced in rice fields dosed with biochar, and the presence of methanophages will increase as the presence of methane increases, leading to a reduction in methane emissions from landfills, and articles say 2.8tonnes per acre biochar dosage results in a drop of methane production from rice paddy fields by 41%. This is best stated as "Methane is bad, adding biochar to methane producing landfills and rice paddies creates less bad".

As stated above, biochar has been proven to minimize the release of methane, which is over 30 (UNEP says 80X) times more potent as a greenhouse gas than carbon dioxide over a 20-100-year period. As biochar enhances the soil structure and water retention capacity, it creates an environment that reduces the production and release of methane, further contributing to climate change mitigation.

As we delve deeper into the impact of biochar on climate change, let's explore its role in slowing down the decomposition of organic matter and preventing the release of methane into the atmosphere whilst locking in carbon dioxide in the form of "inert carbon". A new term has emerged in carbon articles – "inertinite".

Climate change mitigation is becoming an increasingly urgent priority in global environmental efforts, since at the time of writing (Feb 2024) the world temperature is already up against the 1.5°C limit, being quoted as 1.48°C and biochar offers a powerful solution in this arena. By slowing down the decomposition of organic matter and hosting methanophage bacteria, biochar prevents the release of methane into the atmosphere, thus significantly reducing greenhouse gas emissions. This process is not only effective in curbing climate change, but also contributes to the preservation of ecological balance and planetary health. By digging biochar into the soil, we are effectively substituting the CO_2 that the soil would emit as the carbon-based matter decomposes. The real secret is that the Carbon is locked in permanently, does not decompose, so every seasonal dose of biochar increases the amount of carbon dioxide locked underground, and decreases the atmospheric CO_2 levels by 300%. Fast growing biomass like bamboo and elephant grass allow repeated cycling through the year, say every 6-9 months as long as there is a decent % of leafy biomass left above ground to photosynthesize and trap aerial CO_2 into 'wood'. In a 10-year period, 10 cycles of bamboo or elephant grass pyrolyzed and buried as biomass is a "huge negative balance of CO_2 extracted from the air and permanently locked underground per acre".

When organic matter decomposes, it releases carbon dioxide and methane, two potent greenhouse gases that contribute significantly to global warming. By burying Biochar, however, it acts as a natural carbon sink, effectively pre-locking these CO_2 gases away from the atmosphere and reducing the methane emissions to almost zero in the combustion process. This function of biochar is essential in the fight against climate change, offering a practical solution to reduce the impacts of global warming.

In Kenyan villages and farming towns, where the effects of climate change are felt deeply, the role of biochar in preventing the release of harmful gases is especially significant. By implementing biochar as a soil amendment, farmers can slow down the decomposition of organic matter in their fields, thereby reducing their methane and carbon footprint and making a positive impact on the environment.

The use of biochar also has the potential to generate carbon credits, a form of tradeable permit or certificate that provides financial value for every ton of carbon dioxide sequestered or prevented from entering the atmosphere. As the global economy increasingly values carbon credits as a means of mitigating climate change, the role of biochar in this realm becomes even more critical. Kenyan farmers, through the use of biochar, have the opportunity to not only contribute to the reduction of greenhouse gases but also benefit economically from the carbon credits they generate.

In realizing the potential of biochar to mitigate climate change, it's crucial to recognize the ethical and practical aspect of local wealth creation. By empowering farmers to adopt biochar practices, the opportunity for economic growth and sustainability is unlocked within local communities. This not only fosters environmental resilience but also creates a pathway for greater economic prosperity for individuals and families within the region.

The utilization of biochar represents a win-win scenario, where environmentally conscious practices lead to positive economic outcomes. As more farmers and communities adopt biochar techniques, the ripple effect of reduced atmospheric greenhouse gas emissions, lower levels of CO_2 and increased local wealth creation only continues to grow. This highlights the immense potential of biochar to drive positive change and contribute to a more sustainable and prosperous future for all.

The preservation of ecological balance and planetary health is a critical component of biochar's impact on the environment. By mitigating climate change and enhancing soil fertility, biochar plays a central role in promoting a sustainable future for our planet. As we explore the multifaceted benefits of biochar, it becomes evident that its contribution extends beyond environmental protection to encompass economic and social dimensions as well. This holistic approach underscores the profound impact that biochar can have on communities and ecosystems alike.

Carbon Sequestration and Environmental Restoration

Biochar's ability to sequester carbon from the atmosphere by locking it underground for 1,000+ years is a game-changer in the quest to combat climate change. Through carbon farming initiatives in regions from Kisumu to Nairobi to Mombasa, biochar is harnessed to restore degraded lands and enhance soil health whilst lowering atmospheric CO_2. The sequestered carbon not only mitigates greenhouse gas emissions but also fosters the regeneration of natural ecosystems. The positive impact of these efforts reverberates beyond the immediate environment, influencing global carbon credit markets and enhancing biodiversity in these regions whilst removing atmospheric CO_2 and preventing methane escaping into the atmosphere..

Ecosystem Resilience and Community Empowerment

In the face of climate change, biochar not only contributes to ecosystem resilience but also empowers local communities to take charge of their environmental destiny. City dwellers, agriculture, villagers and industries in different countries contribute differently to atmospheric carbon concentrations. However, biochar provides a unifying solution that transcends socioeconomic borders, empowering everyone to actively participate in environmental conservation. This collective effort cultivates a sense of communal responsibility, igniting a passion for safeguarding the natural world and fostering intergenerational stewardship in rural farming communities across this African nation. The extra nutrients in the soil lead to greater abundance of life underground, and with no need for science, a stronger more vibrant soil is better and more resilient all round.

Global Investment Impact and Local Solutions – Thinking out aloud:

In our satellite-internet-blockchain-interconnected world, the significance of foreign investments into local grass-roots solutions cannot be overstated. The paradigm shift that can be facilitated by biochar is inherently rooted in local context and knowledge for production of biochar. As Kenyan villages and rural communities become focal points for biochar production and innovation, an undeniable sense of hope emerges from communities actively engaged in environmental conservation. This firsthand experience of restoration and empowerment becomes a beacon for global sustainability efforts, influencing international discourse and policies related to climate change mitigation and environmental stewardship.

In an ideal world, I would like to see G7 companies from giants like BA, Qantas, Delta, Emirates, to localized bus companies to households buy into biochar burial credits, literally "buried" in a series of designated farms. Security and veracity? Do not rule out the power of the financial markets to cross the sea at lightning speed, with satellite tracking, GPS, real time loading offloading data, blockchain tracking lorries offloading 27-tonne loads of biochar, satellites tracking the soil-carbon % ex-ante and % ex-post the exercise, carbon auditors from E&Y, KPMG, Banks, legal companies, randomised sampling... SGS and Bureau Veritas in Kenya already provide laboratory testing... as will any number of independent soil testing laboratories. (I am reliably informed satellite sensory technology is currently on par with ESP (extra-sensory-perception and Mrs Pink's Medicinal Compound).An investor in G7 should be able to buy the 1 tonne to 1,000 tonne biochar lot securely, knowing that it will be buried on a designated registered farm, and that if he/she were to visit and test the soil, there would be the % increase in soil carbon expected, within error margins. Safe, secure, transparent, able to be audited, and permanent.

Just like any number of auto companies can sell you a vehicle to transport you safely, and you can buy their product, or buy their shares on the LSE, NYSE, there should be a number of such companies listed on NYSE LSE – carbon removal companies – invest in their shares, or buy their "tonnes of CO_2 equivalent removed". The financial rigour being listed on the NYSE and LSE brings trust. (Enron was an anomaly, we will not run a scam, the price we will pay is too high).

Biochar's contribution to the preservation of ecological balance and planetary health exemplifies the transformative potential of sustainable environmental practices. As we delve deeper into the impact of biochar, it becomes clear that its significance transcends local contexts and resonates on a global scale. The collective efforts of rural communities in Kenyan villages to harness biochar for environmental protection is a testament to the power of sustainable solutions in addressing pressing global challenges. The ripple effect of biochar's positive influence on ecosystems and communities is a powerful reminder of the interconnectedness of environmental, economic, and social well-being.

In recognizing biochar's contribution to climate change mitigation, we understand its profound impact on reducing greenhouse gas emissions from soil. This insight into biochar's role in slowing down the decomposition of organic matter and preventing the release of methane into the atmosphere is a critical step toward preserving ecological balance and planetary health. As we conclude this chapter and the entire book, it's important to reflect on the significance of biochar in the larger context of global environmental efforts and its potential for transforming communities and ecosystems in Kenyan rural communities and beyond.

The Potential Impact of Biochar:

Biochar has the potential to revolutionize the way we approach climate change mitigation, natural resource management, and agricultural sustainability. Its role in sequestering carbon underground permanently, improving soil fertility, and reducing greenhouse gas emissions like methane signifies a monumental shift towards a greener and more sustainable future for African communities. It has to be restated: one megatonne of biochar buried is three megatonnes of CO_2 removed.

Leveraging African Biochar for Global Impact:

As we continue to explore the potential of African biochar, we are not only contributing to environmental sustainability locally but also making a significant impact on the global stage. The growing role of carbon credits in the global economy presents an opportunity for African communities to engage in ethical and practical local wealth creation through the production and utilization of biochar. Kenya is already at the two-four megatonne scale for charcoal, it does not take much of an adjustment to reach 10 megatonnes in a few years.

Creating Positive Change Within a Year:

By understanding the potential of biochar and taking actionable steps to leverage its benefits, individuals and communities in Kenya and beyond can make an immediate and long-lasting impact on environmental sustainability. The knowledge and skills gained from this book positions readers to actively contribute to a positive change within a year, without struggling to find comprehensive information.

Fire To Life

Through fervour and deliberate intention, we can enhance ecosystems and uplift the poorest rural communities. It is our commitment to infuse every action with the zeal for a greener future and to wield our knowledge as a powerful tool for positive change.

For the poor, it is more important to be paid. They will as happily replant a forest and guard it as they will to burn it and destroy it. The financial markets play an important role here, as do the regulators and "carbon verification bodies", in linking the richest in world society with the poorest in Kenya and Africa, via the purchasing and sale of carbon credits in their many guises.

As we close this chapter and the book, let's remember that the power to unlock Africa's green potential and contribute to global environmental sustainability lies within each and every one of us. We in Africa will literally grow megatonnes of biomass, char it and bury it, if "you" in G7 and developed countries buy our product. "Trade not Aid".

In harnessing the potential of African biochar for global impact, we not only invest in sustainable practices but also sow the seeds for a brighter and more resilient future. Let's carry the torch of knowledge and act as climate warriors, leading the way towards environmental balance, sustainability, and the well-being of our planet. Know that one tonne of biochar buried in Africa is 3+ tonnes of CO_2 removed from the global atmosphere.

Unveiling Africa's Biochar Potential. Can we reach Gigatonnes per year scale?

One thing is abundantly clear. Africa holds within its soil the key to a sustainable, green future.

I will reiterate: the EU has no spare biomass to speak of, high labour costs, no spare water and certainly no spare land. The USA has billions of tonnes of waste, but very high labour cost and a 10-year wait as courts rule on any mega-project. Africa has billions of tonnes of waste biomass, massive underutilized water resources, spare community/tribal land and a very low labour cost. In any megatonne-scale biochar project, when making the decision as to location, based on logic and financial returns, Africa has to be the logical choice.

With a deep understanding and application of biochar, we can unlock the latent potential of our under-utilized land, cultivate thriving ecosystems, and contribute significantly to global environmental sustainability. It's time to take charge of our collective destiny and harness the power of biochar for the greater good of our planet and all its inhabitants.

This book has delved into the heart of Africa's biochar revolution, unravelling the untapped potential of this invaluable resource. We've explored the intricate web of benefits that biochar offers, from

carbon sequestration to **soil fertility enhancement**, and its pivotal role in enabling sustainable agricultural practices. By analysing real-world applications, we've envisioned a future where biochar becomes an indispensable tool in the fight against climate change and the restoration of our precious ecosystems. By tapping one team of biochar producers, and replicating the systems again and again, (adjusting for local variations) we can reach the gigatonne per year scale for biochar, which is 3gigatonnes per year CO_2 equivalent.

Real-World Applications and Actionable Insights

As we draw our journey to a close, it's essential to consider the practical implications of our newfound knowledge. Readers are encouraged to leverage the insights gained from this book for environmental sustainability efforts in their own lives and work. Whether you're a farmer seeking to enhance crop productivity, a scientist dedicated to mitigating climate change, a family looking to offset your CO_2 emissions, or a policymaker shaping impactful regulations, biochar can be a powerful ally in your noble endeavours.

Recapitulating the Crux of Our Journey

Throughout our odyssey, we've uncovered the manifold benefits of biochar, from its ability to enhance **soil structure** and **nutrient retention** to its unparalleled potential for **carbon sequestration**. We've explored the symbiotic relationship between biochar and indigenous flora, a synergy that holds the key to revitalizing Africa's landscapes and ecosystems. Moreover, we've underscored the undeniable potential for biochar to facilitate not only environmental restoration but also economic empowerment through the creation of local wealth at the lowest economic levels of African society.

Embracing Action for a Sustainable Future

As we bid farewell, it's imperative to acknowledge that our work is far from over. While we've uncovered the transformative potential of biochar, our journey has only just begun. There is a pressing need for further research and exploration in this dynamic field, as we strive to expand our collective knowledge and refine our practices.

Readers are encouraged to seize the reins of change, to employ the principles of biochar with fervour and deliberate intention, and to make informed choices that align with environmental sustainability. Let us embrace the spirit of collaboration and innovation, forging a path towards a future where biochar becomes a cornerstone of environmental restoration and climate change mitigation.

A Memorable Parting Quotation

In parting, let me leave you with a sentiment from our Kenyan Nobel Prize Winner Prof Wangari Maathai, a towering figure in environmental conservation and community empowerment:

Fire To Life

It's the little things citizens do. That's what will make the difference. My little thing is planting trees.
   - ***Wangari Maathai***

As we pave the way for a greener, more sustainable future, let's remember that even the smallest actions can have profound implications. Our collective efforts, guided by the knowledge and wisdom gained from this book, will play a pivotal role in shaping a world where biochar revolutionizes our landscapes, empowers our communities, and safeguards the marvels of our natural world.

Keep the flame of change burning bright, and may the biochar revolution ignite a legacy of environmental stewardship and abundance for generations to come.

"My little thing is making and burying biochar". Nawaz Khan.

Technical Notes

1) When we say "biochar for burying in the ground", it is ALWAYS charged by mixing it with manure, animal urine and composted plant matter, between 30% to 40% by weight. Charged biochar is beneficial immediately. By comparison, uncharged biochar takes 12-24 months to become beneficial. When we say 10 tonnes of biochar, we are only referring to the weight of the charcoal, the manure, urine and compost is disregarded.

2) When we say "villages surrounding the cities" we mean that the big cities are a massive source of food and industrial waste that can be charred, and transport distances need to be minimised to keep the carbon footprint low. These villages and communities can also grow biomass for the purpose of being buried as biochar, be it bamboo, fast growing grasses or fast growing woody weeds. Lastly, these cities are massive markets for the food crops grown in these villages. In any biochar project, minimizing transport distances and hence carbon footprint and expenses is an important consideration for the next 10 years, till solarized e-logistics becomes a reality.

Successful Case Studies:

I have to apologize here – I do not really know of any successful field studies outside of a laboratory/field study in Kenya. By this I mean real farmers, real crops, Ceteris Paribus. The Kenyan companies selling biochar I know are new. India is our bigger brother here – and far more advanced down the path than we are, albeit by a year or two.

The reader can take comfort from the fact that 100% of what grows in India is grown in Kenya – courtesy of the Indians imported to build the railway 130-odd years ago. All the locally grown Indian vegetables in Kenya, are exported to UK for the Indian immigrant population there, so quality is comparable, if not superior. (Except rice).

The aforementioned Study by Sweden's Lund University (2019-09-25) was startling in its improvement: At the site located in Kwale (Kenya's Coast province) the yield increases of maize showed a strong positive correlation with biochar dose. In the first season, yields increased from 900Kg per hectare in the control plot to 4.4 tonnes per hectare in average in the biochar-amended plots. 480% plus improvement seems too good to be true, I think the farm had multiple faults corrected by the biochar.

In Siaya, Western Kenya a region known for badly depleted soils (and stunted inbred animals), an average biochar dose of 2,800Kg per hectare lead to an increase in maize yields from 2,900Kg to

Fire To Life

3,800Kg per hectare in average in the first season and from 1,700Kg to 2,500 Kg per hectare in the second season after biochar addition.

But let us examine "real farmers on the ground with budget restrictions in real life".

Case Study1: Farm Location: Lonkheda, Shahada District, India.

Crop Chickpeas, Variety PKV2. 50% of the field is dosed with biochar, 50% remains as per normal. On target for 40% improvement in biochar dosed field.

Case Study2: Farm Location: Rohtas District, India.

Crop Rice, field is dosed with biochar, Achieved 40% improvement in biochar dosed field.

Case Study3: Farm Location: Rohtas District, India.

Crop Wheat, field is dosed with biochar, expecting 40% improvement in biochar dosed field.

*Case studies 1,2,and 3 are from Varhad Capital, who make biochar in India. Case studies quoted with kind permission from Prasad Dahapute, CEO.

Case Study4:

8 field sites, Nepal. Case studies here – were done by Itaka Institute of Switzerland, using real farmers. Some of the results are counter-intuitive, but very promising. There were 3 different field tests, all included cow manure:

Treatment1: Cow manure plus Urine. Treatment2: Cow manure plus biochar only. Treatment3: Urine+ Biochar. All at 750Kg per Ha.

Result1: Manure + Urine = 20.4 tonnes per Ha

Result2: Manure + Biochar = 44.6 tonnes per Ha

Result3: Manure + Biochar + Urine = 82.6 tonnes per Ha.

Full details available at: Fourfold Increase in Pumpkin Yield in Response to Low-Dosage

Root Zone Application of Urine-Enhanced Biochar to a Fertile Tropical Soil

Hans Peter Schmidt 1,*, Bishnu Hari Pandit 2, Vegard Martinsen 3, Gerard Cornelissen 3,4,5,

Pellegrino Conte 6, Claudia I. Kammann Agriculture 2015, 5, 723-741; doi:10.3390/agriculture5030723

Printed in Great Britain
by Amazon